Prolonged employment of older workers.
Determinants of managers' decisions regarding hiring,
retention and training

PROLONGED EMPLOYMENT OF OLDER WORKERS

Determinants of managers' decisions
regarding hiring, retention and training

Kasia Karpinska

netherlands
interdisciplinairy
demographic
institute

N i D i

Book 89

Koninklijke Nederlandse Akademie van Wetenschappen

Routledge
Taylor & Francis Group

LONDON AND NEW YORK

The series of NIDI reports is published by the Netherlands
Interdisciplinairy Demographic Institute

First published in 2013 by Amsterdam University Press Ltd.

Published 2025 by Routledge
4 Park Square, Milton Park, Abingdon, Oxon OX14 4RN
605 Third Avenue, New York, NY 10158

Routledge is an imprint of the Taylor & Francis Group, an informa business

ISBN: 9789069846668 (pbk)
ISBN: 9781003702061 (ebk)
ISSN 0922-7210

For Product Safety Concerns and Information please contact our EU
representative: GPSR@taylorandfrancis.com
Taylor & Francis Verlag GmbH, Kaufingerstraße 24, 80331 München,
Germany

Table of contents

1. General introduction

1.1. Introduction

This dissertation focuses on attitudes and behaviour of managers towards older workers. With an application of vignette studies questions of what factors that affect the hiring of early retirees (*i.e.* workers who retired before the mandatory retirement age of 65 and receive pre-retirement benefits), training opportunities of older workers and their retention are evaluated. Prolonged and productive employment of older workers is seen as a necessary condition to maintain welfare and social security systems threatened by ageing populations. Despite this importance, the labour market position of older workers is much worse than that of workers in primal age (Conen, Henkens and Schippers, 2011). The general goal of this dissertation is to increase our understanding of the labour market participation of older workers and factors that affect it.

Employment of workers around retirement age has become more dynamic over the past decades. Retirement used to be characterised as a definite and abrupt exit from the workforce after a long working career (Hardy, 2002). Recently however, it has come to be seen as a more gradual transition from a working to a non-working life. Early retirement, part-time retirement or re-entry into the labour force, form possible paths of transition transitions between the labour force and retirement that are available for older workers (Henkens, Van Solinge and Van Dalen; 2013: Hardy, 2002). The dynamics in the labour market for older workers are determined by workers' preferences towards preferred level of occupational activity and their behaviours and are also affected by the restrictions that workers face on the labour market and possibilities open in organisations. The current study evaluates which individual characteristics of older workers, organisations and managers affect decisions to hire older workers, offer them training opportunities and retain them in organisations.

Insights into older workers' labour market participation and factors that affect it are of great importance for both scientific and societal reasons. From a scientific perspective, this study increases our understanding of various aspects of older workers' employment; it examines decisions that managers take with respect to early retirees' re-entry into the labour force as well as older workers' retention in organisations and their exit from the labour market. The academic community has focused extensively on organisational policies with respect to older workers' employment (Conen *et al.*, 2011), but only limited attention has been paid to specific decisions that managers take when hiring, training and retaining older workers and the factors that affect these decisions. The questions of what specific circumstances affect older workers' chances to prolong their productive employment have been scarce. This study fills that gap and examines how various characteristics of older workers affect employers' decisions.

Moreover, the present study suggests that older workers' hiring, training opportunities and retention are also influenced by the images that managers hold about older workers. Shultz and Henkens (2010) suggested that the success of policies aimed at delaying retirement is to a large extent dependent on the actions and attitudes of employers. The evidence suggests that employers are not very positive about extending of older workers' careers and that these negative attitudes can form barriers to employment (Loretto and White, 2006; Taylor and Walker, 1998a). Although many scientists suggest that ageist attitudes affect decisions towards older workers (Chui, Chan, Snape and Redman, 2001), to date only limited attention has been paid to estimating the effect of such attitudes on decisions to hire, train or retain older workers. With a combination of survey data and vignette studies carried out in 2010 among managers in Dutch organisations, this dissertation investigates the impact of attitudes on employment decisions of managers. The approach helps increase our understanding of how attitudes affect the likelihood of hiring, training opportunities and retention of older workers.

Furthermore, studying factors that affect managers' employment decisions with respect to older workers bears societal importance. First, prolonged and productive employment of older workers has significant repercussions at the macro level; workers who remain active or return to the labour force contribute longer to the welfare state and social security systems, and help maintaining their sustainability. This is an important issue in the light of shifts in the population structure and an ageing workforce.

Secondly, organisations too can benefit from the knowledge of how the various employment decisions are taken. This study increases our understanding of how general policies towards older workers are embodied in organisational practice. Moreover, this study sheds light on the role of managers' images on employment decisions, an issue that has been discussed by many scholars in the field of age discrimination (Chui *et al.*, 2006; Loretto and White, 2006).

A third reason for studying such decisions and their determinants has to do with older workers themselves. Many older workers intend to postpone their retirement while others try to re-enter the labour market. Those trends will most likely increase in the near future. Knowledge of how organisations manage older workers and their employability can help workers not only identifi the chances and possibilities in the labour market, but also to prepare for their extended employment and foresee potential barriers.

Before formulating the aims and research questions in greater detail, I will focus on the demographic changes and labour force participation trends in the Netherlands (section 1.2). Next, I will present previous research on employment of older workers and the role of general attitudes in that process (section 1.3). This will be followed by a discussion on some theoretical considerations concerning the decisionmaking process (section 1.4). The methods and research design will be discussed in section 1.5, while the final section of this chapter gives a brief overview of the outline of this book.

1.2. Ageing and labour market participation in the Netherlands

1.2.1.   Demographic developments
Many European societies face a process of ageing of their populations and the Netherlands is not an exception. The demographic transformation is to be accounted for by the drop in fertility rates on the one hand and increasing life expectancy on the other. *Figures 1.1* and *1.2* picture the changes that have occurred in the Netherlands in the previous century. Figure 1.1 portrays the development of total fertility rates in the Netherlands. It shows that after the 1960s and the introduction of the pill as a method of contraception fertility rates dropped dramatically, which is similar to trends observed in other Western European countries. Demographers predict that from approximately the year 2000 fertility has been stabilizing at the level of 1.8 children per woman (Van Nimwegen, Beets, Schoorl and Ekamper, 2011).

Figure 1.2 portrays the development of life expectancy in the Netherlands and shows that since the 1960s life expectancy for both men and women has been constantly increasing. Statistics Netherlands predicts it expectancy will further increase and projects that around 2060 it will reach the level of 84.5 years for males and 87.3 years for females (Statistics Netherlands, 2012a).

Figure 1.1. Total fertility rates in the Netherlands, 1960-2060

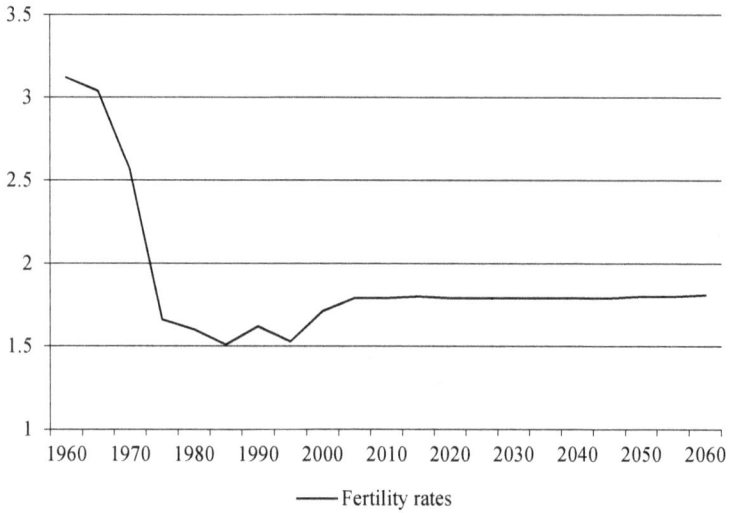

Note: Statistics for the period 1960-2010 are retrieved from Eurostat's Demography Database (2012); Projections for the period 2015-2060 are retrieved from EUROPOP2010 (2012). More about methodology at http://epp.eurostat.ec.europa.eu/

Figure 1.2. Life expectancy at birth in the Netherlands, 1960-2060

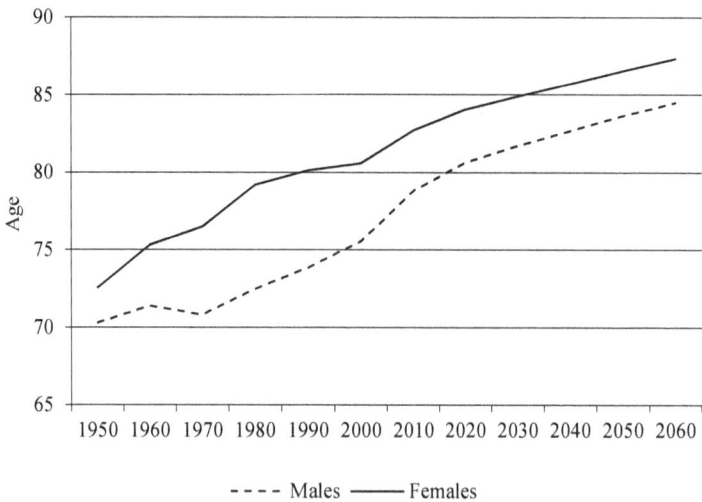

Source: Statistics Netherlands, 2012a.

Low fertility rates, combined with increasing life expectancy lead to shifts in the demographic structure of the Dutch population and causes its ageing. The number of older people (age 65 and older) is predicted to increase substantially from 2.6 millions in 2010 to 4.6 million in 2040. The number of people aged 20-64 had been constantly rising until the year 2000, when it reached a level of approximately 10 million and remained at this level for the next two decades. After 2020, this number decreases slightly and is expected to stabilise at the level of 9.5 million after 2040. *Figure 1.3* pictures those changes and shows an increasing share of older people in the Dutch population over the years (Statistics Netherlands, 2012b; c).

These demographic changes will have significant consequences for the welfare state and the labour market. The generation of baby boomers in the Netherlands, *i.e.* those born shortly after World War II, started leaving the labour force in 2010 and will be entering retirement up to approximately 2015. Consequently, an increasing number of older people will claim their old-age pensions and more will depend on health care, increasing public expenditures on the health care system. Enlarging the pool of productive workers, in terms of their labour market participation levels and extending their working life, is seen as a key element for dealing with increasing welfare state expenditures (Ministry of Social Affairs and Employment, 2011).

1.2.2. Changes in labour market policies
Increasing the labour market participation of older workers has become apparent at both the European and the national level. The 1994 EU summit was the first to stress the need to improve employment opportunities for older workers. Shortly after that, in 2000 the Lisbon European Council set the strategic goals for the development of employment rates in the European Union. The target was set at reaching a 50 percent employment rate for older workers (aged 55-64), a significant increase from the European average of 26.3 percent in the year 2000 (European Commission, 2010).

Labour market polices in the Netherlands have been transformed over the last three decades. In the early 1980s early exits schemes (VUT) were introduced as a remedy against high youth unemployment. Those schemes were fairly generous (with replacement rates of 80 percent) and were financed on a pay-as-you-go basis. Furthermore, disincentives to continue working beyond the age of 55 have been enhanced by the availability of unemployment and disability schemes (Kapteyn and De Vos, 1998). In fact, in 1998 nearly one-third of men in the age category 55 to 64 received disability benefits (Centraal Planbureau (CBP), 2000).

Figure 1.3. Number of people aged 25-65, 65 and older and 80 and older, 1950-2060 (in millions)

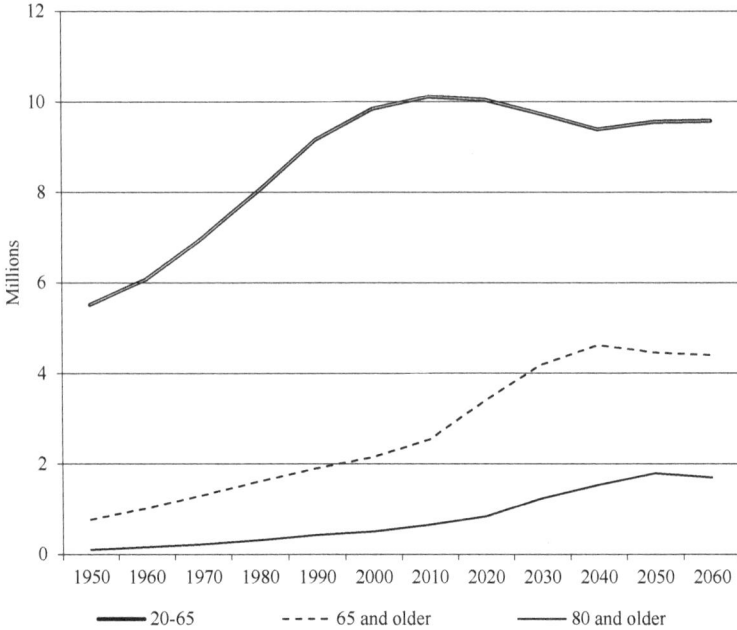

Source: Statistics Netherlands, 2012b; c.

Since the 1990s, it has become apparent that these early retirement schemes are not sustainable, as they form a threat to social security systems; due to the ageing of the population higher numbers of workers exited the labour force early, increasing the expenditures of social security. At that point the policy focus was switched from encouragement of early retirement to encouragement of working longer (Van Dalen and Henkens, 2002). Early exit schemes have been restricted and the age at which older workers are eligible for early retirement has been raised while compensation levels have decreased. At the same time, financial incentives for working longer have been introduced and access to alternative exits routes (unemployment or disability schemes) has been restricted.

In 2006 another change of policies took place and pre-pension schemes (VUT) were further sharpened. The polices introduced over the past two decades have resulted in increasing labour market participation; older workers retire now later than they used to. *Figure 1.4* shows that while workers in 2001

Figure 1.4. Average retirement age in the Netherlands, 2003-2011

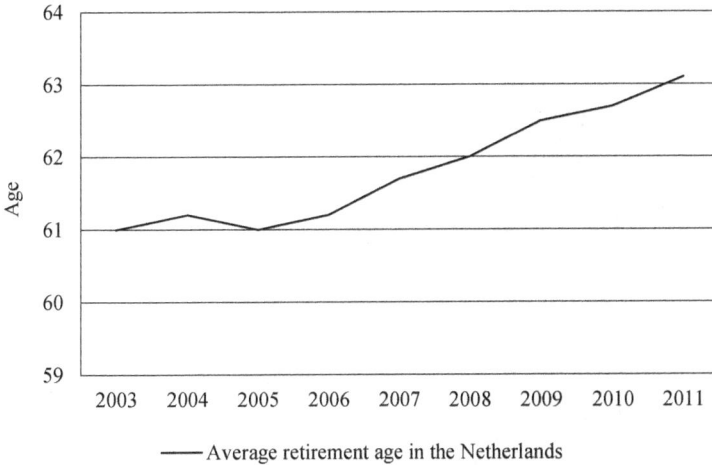

—— Average retirement age in the Netherlands

Source: Statistics Netherlands, 2012d.

retired on average when they reached the age of 61, after 2006 an increase in the exit age was observed. In 2011 the average retirement age was 63 (Statistics Netherlands, 2012d). A recent policy change introduces a stepwise increase of the public pension age. Starting in 2013 the retirement age will be raised to 66 years and will reach 67 in 2024. After that, the retirement age will be interlinked with life expectancy (Government of the Netherlands, 2012).

As stated earlier, retirement can be characterised as a process that can take multiple forms such as early retirement, part-time retirement or even re-entry into the labour force (Hardy, 2002; Wang Zhan, Liu and Shultz, 2008). In the Netherlands those possibilities are embedded in various polices that aim at increasing older workers' participation in the labour force. Hence in most cases re-entry of (early) retirees is not restricted by labour force regulations or law, as employers can hire older worker even after the age of 65. This policy also allows for a certain amount of additional income for early retirees with no risk of losing early pension benefits (Van Dalen, Henkens, Lokhorst and Schippers, 2009).

Figure 1.5 pictures the change in labour market participation of early retirees between 2002 and 2007 and shows that an increasing number of early retirees either entered paid employment (of one hour per week or more) or expressed

*Figure 1.5. Percentage of early retirees employed or willing to find employment,
2002-2007*

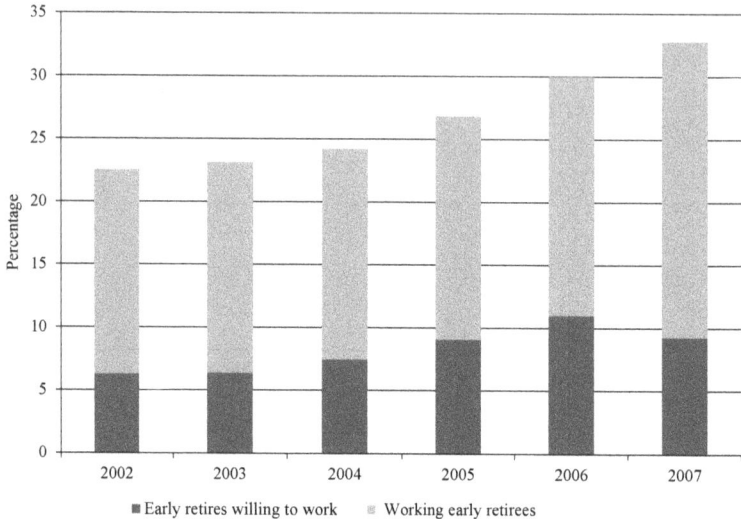

Source: Van Dalen *et al.*, 2009.

the willingness to do so. In 2002, 16 percent of early retirees were employed, and approximately 6 percent indicated they would be willing to re-enter the labour market. In 2007 both labour market participation and intentions to participate increased; 23 percent of early retirees were employed, while 10 percent had this ambition but were not employed (Van Dalen *et al.*, 2009).

Next to incentives for older workers, also tax policies have been introduced to stimulate employers to hire older workders (Euwals, De Mooij and Van Vuuren, 2009). Organisations that retain workers older than 62 can apply discounted social security premiums (Rijksoverheid, 2012). Also, tax deductions were introduced for organisations that hire workers older than age 50. This initiative aimed to stimulate reintegration of the long term unemployed (*i.e.* workers who had been searching for a new position for longer than 12 months). Various sources indicate that unemployment among this category of workers is increasing (in 2011 almost 40 percent of the unemployed were older than 45, Statistics Netherlands, 2012c) and older workers face the lowest chances of finding new employment (UVW, 2012).

Changes in different policies have resulted in increasing labour market participation of older workers. *Figure 1.6* pictures the changes in the labour

Figure 1.6. Nett labour market participation of workers aged 55-64, the Netherlands, 1996-2011

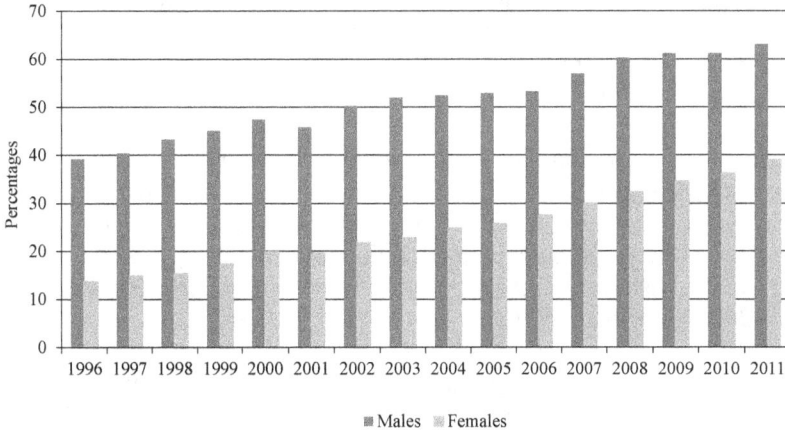

Source: Statistics Netherlands, 2012e.

market participation of both male and female workers aged 55 to 64 between 1996 and 2011 (Statistics Netherlands, 2012e). While in 1996 less than 40 percent of men and about 14 percent of women aged 55-64 were employed, these numbers increased substantially by the year 2011. At that time, more than 60 percent of males were employed and female participation doubled to reach 38 percent.

This increasing participation can be attributed to the policy adjustments but also to cohort effects. Current cohorts of older workers are more highly educated than earlier cohorts from several decades ago, and these higher educated cohorts are more inclined to participate in the workforce. Also, an increasing number of women are employed and prolong their employment (Van Doorne-Huiskes and Schippers, 2010). Importantly, current older workers are employed in less physically demanding jobs, and in combination with a general trend of improving health and better health care they are also able to carry on their occupational responsibilities longer (Johnson, 2009).

To further increase the labour market participation of older workers more attention has been paid in recent years to the issue of worker employability. A new set of policies proposed by the Dutch Government, the so-called Vitality Package, stresses the importance of lifelong learning and points out that both (older) workers and organisations are responsible for maintaining workers employability over the course of their employment (Ministry of Social Affairs and Employment, 2011). Specific policy initiatives include a training account, *i.e.* a budget for the retraining in case of (impending) unemployment. At the same time organisations are expected to participate in from-work-to-work funds that will help retrain workers and prepare them for employment in a different sector.

The necessity of lifelong learning is not yet visible in training participation rates. On average, about 16 percent of all workers in the Netherlands participated in training activities in 2009 (Statistics Netherlands, 2012f), yet, older workers' participation in training is considerably lower. *Figure 1.7* displays the distribution of the lifelong learning participation rates for the years 2000, 2005 and 2009.

In all presented years, the youngest workers (between ages 20 and 30) were trained most often and their participation rates varied between 26 and 31 percent. Training participation decreased for each consecutive age category. In 2009 the participation rate for workers aged 50-55 was 13 percent and only 10 percent of workers between ages 55 and 60 received training. In 2009 the

Figure 1.7. Lifelong training participation for different age categories, 2000-2009

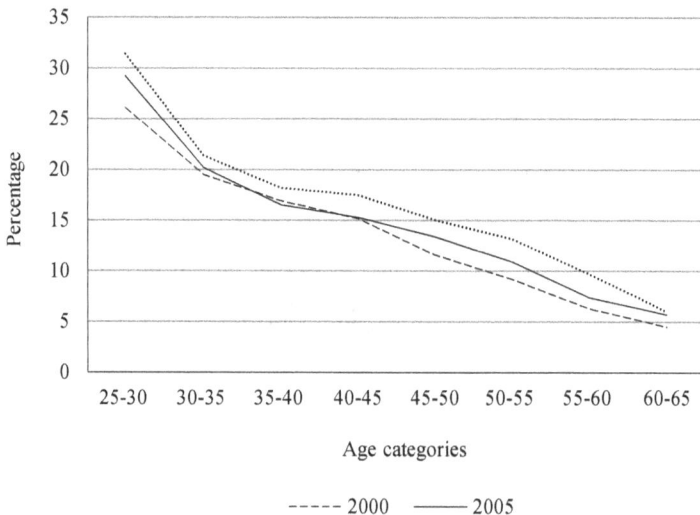

Source: Statistics Netherlands, 2012f.

oldest workers between ages 60 and 65, were offered training opportunities at the lowest rate, as only 6 percent of them followed training. Still, those numbers were slightly higher than in 2002.

1.3.   Previous research on older workers' employment

The process of retirement and (productive) employment at later ages depends greatly on the demand for older workers. Various studies indicate that managers strongly influence the employment of older workers around retirement. Henkens (1999) and Van Solinge and Henkens (2007) have shown that in their decision to postpone early retirement workers take into account the opinion of their direct managers; older workers retire later if their manager supports continued employment. Employers define the opportunities for prolonged employment, training or labour market re-entry for early retirees. It had been suggested that the lack of support for employment may reflect underlying attitudes that older workers can offer less to organisations than younger workers (McCann and Giles, 2002). Age discrimination is pictured to be one of the forces behind low labour market participation of older workers.

To gain more knowledge about employers' attitudes and behaviours towards older workers, a growing body of evidence has been collected. Two strains of literature can be identified. First, several studies have applied survey methods to examine employers', managers' and human resource managers' opinions and practices towards older workers. Those survey studies have provided valuable data on support for government initiatives to work longer and were conducted both in the Netherlands (Henkens, 2005; Van Dalen *et al.*, 2009; 2010a) and in other countries dealing with ageing their populations (*c.f.* Conen, 2012). The studies report findings with respect to stereotypical views of older workers and organisational policies towards them (Taylor and Walker, 1998a; Conen *et al.*, 2011). Survey results show that support for later retirement is relatively low among employers in the Netherlands (Conen, Henkens and Schippers, 2011). Evidence from Germany indicates that managers are still more likely to retain older workers than to recruit them (Daniel and Heywood, 2007), suggesting limited chances of early retirees to re-enter the workforce.

The second important strain of literature focused on decision-making and applied mostly experimental settings (factorial experiments, in-basket or audit studies). These studies examined factors that influence selection and hiring (Avolio and Barrett, 1987; Dedrick and Dobbins, 1991; Bendick, Jackson and Romero, 1997; Singer and Sewell, 1989), training, retention or retirement recommendation (Rosen, Jerdee and Lunn, 1981) and promotions (Shore, Cleveland and Goldberg, 2003). These studies report what contextual factors affect decisions regarding older workers (*i.e.* job related information, cognitive strain of the raters and salience of the experimental conditions; Finkelstein, Burke and Raju, 1995; Finkelstein and Burke, 1998; Perry, Kulik and Bourhis, 1996) and confirm that older workers were assessed less positively than younger subjects (*i.e.* a person that is subject to the decisions) in virtually all employment decisions, suggesting the presence of an age bias.

Although surveys and experimental studies have increased our understanding of managers' policies and behaviours on the one hand and decision-making on the other, they both have some limitations. Survey studies focus on employer policies on older workers as a general category but do not provide insights into who gets training and who does not. Similarly, those studies do not evaluate what specific characteristics of older workers affect the likelihood of retention or hiring. The studies do not provide an empirical test of the relation between attitudes and behaviours either.

Experimental research often studies decisions towards older workers who are described by their age, and only a limited number of other characteristics of older workers are included in the experimental settings (Dedrick and Dobbins, 1991; Bendick *et al.*, 1997). It is therefore difficult to draw conclusions on which characteristics of older workers stimulate hiring, training opportunities or retention, or what settings endorse those decisions. Moreover, age of older workers is often treated as a proxy of age-related attitudes; those studies do not include other measures of ageist attitudes. Although it has been suggested that both stereotypes and age norms may affect employers' behaviour (Chiu *et al.*, 2001; Finkelstein and Burke, 1998; Lee and Clemons, 1985; Loretto, Duncan and White, 2000), not much empirical evidence has been presented to support this connection. Consequently, drawing conclusions on the impact of those attitudes on behaviour is impossible. Last but not least, those studies often use students as surrogates for managers. Although it is often claimed that students are future managers, many studies applying student samples suggest replication of the results with manger samples (Dedrick and Dobbins, 1991; Perry and Bourhis, 1996), arguing that students' samples lack essential experience for the decisions taken as a part of the experimental design (Remus, 1996). This, in turn, supposedly limits the generalisability of the results (Hitt and Barr, 1996).

The current study bridges the two strains of literature and applies a design that combines the advantages of survey data and experimental study (*i.e.* vignette study). While the survey offers the possibility to collect information on managers' attitudes towards older workers, vignette design facilitates modelling the decisions that managers take with respect to specific older workers. Combined, this data allows empirical testing of the impact of various characteristics of older workers and organisations on managers' decisions and also extends previous studies by testing empirically the effect managers' general attitudes have on their decisions.

1.4. Theoretical perspectives

Different disciplines of social sciences present fundamentally similar models explaining human behaviour. The basic assumption is that human actions are guided by the principle of rationality: One acts in a way that yields the greatest benefits. This assumption is present in theories of rational choice in economics, social exchange in sociology and decision-making in psychology (Marini, 1992). Yet, there are several differences in how the various disciplines specify their models. Economists propose that people are guided by preferences, which are generally stable over time and uniform for all people, and people that strive towards their maximisation, bounded by a set of restrictions.

Becker (1957) extended the economic framework and suggested that although preferences are stable over time, they can differ between persons. He applied this assumption to problems of the labour market and suggested that employers, employees and customers may have specific tastes on who they are not willing associate with. Those tastes can lead to discrimination in the labour market as the subject of the discriminatory attitudes will not be hired or will be hired only against lower wages. Becker interpreted differential positions of persons and groups as an indicator for discriminatory behaviours, given that all other conditions (*e.g.* worker productivity) were equal. Differences in behavioural outcomes (discriminatory behaviour or lack of thereof) are assumed to indicate differences in how people perceive others.

Economic theory predicts that although humans are striving towards maximisation of their preferences, those preferences cannot be fully realized due to the restrictions, *i.e.* elements of the context that influence the possibilities of certain actions. This point is accentuated by the sociological individualistic tradition, which recognises that human actions are indeed rational, but this is rather an 'as if' rationality: It can take different forms and depends on the context, which defines possibilities and restrictions of the actions available for actors. Consequently, human actions are always understandable within that context (Boudon, 1987).

In line with this logic, the context and constraints present within that context shape the possibilities for managers to act according to their preferences. Employment decisions regarding older workers will be contingent on the possibilities present in organisations and the characteristics of older workers who are subject to those decisions. Managers represent organisations and are supposed to contribute towards organisational goals by realising high production levels and low costs, reduced absenteeism and good social relations and by nurturing good sources of knowledge and contacts (Kalleberg, Knoke, Marsden and Spaeth, 1996). Similarly, achievement of organisational goals depends on the recruitment and maintenance of qualified staff (Kalleberg et al., 1996). In their decisions managers also take into account characteristics of older workers as these imply whether specific employment choices are desirable or not. Attributes that will be evaluated might differ per situation and can include older workers' human capital, physical and mental health status, work attitudes, et cetera.

This study aims to integrate the analysis of both preferences and restrictions that managers face, and evaluate their role in hiring, training opportunities and retention decisions regarding older workers. The framework of this study is defined by rational economic theory and extended with insights from sociology and social psychology. Tazelaar (1982) argued that much sociological research sheds light on the influences of restrictions and resources on decisions, but does not examine the role that cognition and affections play in that process. At the same time, in social psychological research much attention is paid to the influence of the mental systems while neglecting the relationship between different contexts and behaviours. In the current study two aspects of the mental system are considered, namely stereotypes and age norms. Norms are defined as rules that coordinate interactions with others and are believed to guide individuals in social situations (Coleman, 1990; Liefbroer and Billari, 2010). Stereotypes have been described as 'beliefs about the characteristics, attributes and behaviours of members of certain groups (...) and beliefs about how and why those attributes go together' (Hilton and Von Hippel, 1996, p. 240). There is a wide body of literature that focuses on the general attitudes of employers towards older workers and suggests that those attitudes frame managers' perceptions of older workers and their abilities (Chiu *et al.*, 2001; Finkelstein and Burke, 1998; Loretto *et al.*, 2000; Van Dalen *et al.*, 2010b).

To date, various studies have focused either on preferences (*i.e.* attitudes managers' have towards older workers) or restrictions (*i.e.* policies affecting older workers and the impact of the supply side on employment decisions), yet hardly any study hascombined the two paths. Moreover, the present study applies this framework to examine the decisions of entry, employment and exit from the labour force of older workers, thus offering a comprehensive view of the employment dynamics for workers around retirement age and factors that affect it.

1.5. Methods

1.5.1. Research design
In the evaluation of the factors that affect managers' employment decisions towards older workers this study applies data that was collected in 2010 and consists of a combination of survey research with a factorial study. The data was collected by accessing the sample of the LISS panel (Longitudinal Internet Studies for the Social Sciences of Tilburg University, http://www.lissdata. nl/lissdata/). LISS is an Internet panel that consists of 5.000 households, comprising 8.000 individuals. All individuals were selected based on a true probability sample of households drawn from the population register by Statistics Netherlands. The data was collected in two stages: first a survey was administered to managers and questions regarding the characteristics of respondents and their perception of age norms and stereotypes were asked. One month later the same managers were approached again to complete a vignette study.

The monthly gap introduced in the design was based on methodological considerations. Firstly, questions about stereotypes are sensitive in nature. If both studies were combined and executed at the same time, earlier questions on attitudes might have primed respondents, leading to biased results. Although we can never exclude the possibility of bias introduced by asking the same respondents questions about a similar matter, the monthly gap limited the risk of bias related to potential carryover effects (Leeuw, Hox and Dillman, 2008).

Also, in this study design we followed the suggestion put forward by Liefbroer and Billari (2010): to properly analyse the effect of norms on behaviour the perception of norms needs to be observed before the actual behaviour. The same applies to stereotypes. In our study those attitudes are treated as a given, and measured before vignettes measuring decisions are introduced. This semi-panel design is well-suited to analyse the effect of stereotypes and norms on (hypothetical) behaviour.

1.5.2.   Vignettes design

A vignette study (also called factorial survey) is a method intended for the investigation of human actions and judgments that are difficult to measure (Rossi and Anderson, 1982). The basic item of the factorial survey is a vignette, which is a short description of a situation or a person generated by combining characteristics randomly manipulated by the researcher (Ganong and Coleman, 2006; Wallander, 2009). Vignettes are defined by a number of factors and their respective dimensions constitute a so-called *vignette universe*, *i.e.* all possible combinations of the factors applied. In contrast with a factorial experiment in which all possible combinations are evaluated, in a factorial survey only a random selection from the universe of vignettes is judged by respondents (Wallander, 2009). This allows for a larger number of vignette dimensions and levels to be included in the design, enhancing resemblance between the experimental and the real worlds (Rossi and Anderson, 1982) and assuring are greater reality than laboratory experiments. Yet, an important requirement is that the number of characteristics be restricted because participants typically are unable to process large amounts of information. If too many dimensions are introduced, it becomes difficult for the participant to visualise the hypothetical situation clearly (Rossi and Anderson, 1982). Vignette approach is often characterised as a hybrid technique, as it combines the factor orthogonality (perfect non-association between dimensions) with the rich detail and complexity that may be obtained using sample survey procedures (Wallander, 2009; Ganong and Coleman, 2006).

There are several general advantages of using of a vignette design. First, presenting respondents with concrete and detailed descriptions of the situation or a person, this approach offers the possibility to study context and conditions affecting judgments (Wallander, 2009). Second, advocates of this method suggest that respondents in a factorial survey are unaware of the manipulation of various factors in the vignette and therefore, are supposedly less susceptible to social desirability bias. Finally, Wallander (2009) points out that people are usually not aware of the factors that influence their judgment and are not able to name them when asked about them explicitly.

Application of vignette surveys helps disentangle the determinants of human judgments and actions.

The advantages of a vignette design are recognised in many areas of the social sciences (for an overview see Wallander, 2009), and this method was applied earlier in the evaluation of employment outcomes. Jacobs *et al.* (1990) applied vignette surveys to study the hiring of women for positions in the police force. Van Beek *et al.* (1997) looked at managers' propensity to hire different unemployed job seekers while de Wolf and Van der Velden (2001) assessed employment chances of social science graduates in different types of academic positions. Henkens, Van Solinge and Cozijnsen (2009) applied the vignette approach to study retention of older workers in the Netherlands.

1.5.3.   Respondents
To gain insight into the hiring, training and retention decisions with respect to older workers, data on managers was needed. Many studies that examine employment decisions utilise students as surrogates for managers. The argument here is that students, especially those in business courses, are future managers and their coursework already prepares them for the role of managers. The ongoing debate in many social science disciplines questions the external validity of the results based on student samples (Barr and Hitt, 1996). Those studies suggest that students' perceptions would rarely be appropriate as a basis for examining significant managerial issues, and generalisation to the broader population of practicing managers is therefore inappropriate (Barr and Hitt, 1996; Das, 2003). Students' samples are claimed to lack essential experience for the decisions they take as a part of experimental design (Remus, 1996). In their comparison between how managers and students evaluate retention decisions of older workers, Henkens *et al.* (2009) showed that although students did not differ much in the decisions they took, they were less influenced by the organisational context than experienced managers.

Clearly, decisions of managers with respect to older workers require some experience in decision-making. The focus on managers is thus a prerequisite for improving external validity of the results. While there are many studies in organisational and industrial psychology that use an experimental design with student sample to evaluate employment chances and outcomes for older workers, most of them suggest that their results need to be corroborated with a managers' sample (Dedrick and Dobbins, 1991; Perry *et al.*, 1996).

1.6. Outline of the book

To answer our general research question on decisions that managers take with respect to older workers, we will pose four more specific research questions that refer to different aspects of employment and the impact of managers' general attitudes on those decisions. Chapters 2 to 5 present the results of the study. These chapters were written as separate journal articles. Two chapters have been published (Chapter 2 and 3). Presenting the results of the study in the form of articles has an advantage that each chapter can be read independently. One disadvantage of this approach is that certain overlap may occur, especially when considering the method applied in the study.

The first two chapters focus on decisions that managers take with respect to hiring early retirees. Chapter 2 takes the initial step towards an understanding of those decisions, and looks at choices that both managers and business students take when presented with the profiles of hypothetical early retirees. This study is based on data collected at the Dutch Interdisciplinary Demographic Institute (NIDI) in March 2009, within the framework of a project executed for the Raad voor Werk en Inkomen (RWI, for details see Van Dalen et al., 2009). While managers often participate in surveys or focus groups meetings (Truss, 2001; Hailey, Farndale and Truss, 2005), they traditionally prove difficult to reach and unwilling to participate in experimental research (Remus, 1996). Additionally, the study was also conducted among business students of Utrecht University. This data consist of only the vignette study and was used as a pilot before the main data collection took place.

In Chapter 3 I replicate the results of the first study and extend the analysis by also modelling the effect of managers' images and attitudes on their hiring decisions. This study applies the data that consists of a survey and a vignette study collected by accessing the members of the LISS panel survey. The sample consisted of managers only. All remaining chapters draw on this data source.

Chapter 4 focuses on factors that affect older workers' training opportunities and the impact of age norms on those opportunities. Among other factors, the effect of age norms is also evaluated. In the last empirical chapter the focus lies on retention of older workers. The analysis is extended by looking not only at the impact of age norms on managers' decisions but also at their stereotypical views of older workers' productivity. Chapter 6 summarises the main findings of the study and evaluates the answers to the specific research questions and discusses the relevance of this study.

2. The recruitment of early retirees: a vignette study of the factors that affect managers' decisions[1]

2.1. Introduction

Retirement used to be characterised as a definite and abrupt exit from the work force after a long working career (Hardy, 2002). Recently however, retirement has come to be seen as a more dynamic and gradual transition from a working to a non-working life, where deliberate choices are made with respect to timing of retirement and preferred level of occupational activity (Wang *et al.*, 2008). This more dynamic process is protracted and leads to different outcomes: From early retirement through part-time retirement to re-entry into the labour force, depending on the specific regulations that apply (Hardy, 2002). Recent studies indicate that a substantial number of early retirees (*i.e.* older workers who leave the labour force before the mandatory retirement age) re-enter the work force after early retirement (Henkens, Van Dalen and Van Solinge, 2009). The reasons for re-entering the labour market are diverse: A need for social contacts and recognition as well as financial needs may be important elements of the aspiration to remain active in the labour market (Kim and Feldman, 2000; Wang *et al.*, 2008). While older workers have some agency about whether to retire from work or to enter self employment (Bruce, Holtz-Eakin and Quinn, 2000), retired workers' prospects of returning to the labour force are largely determined by employers and the availability of jobs in organisations (Henkens, Van Dalen and Van Solinge, 2009). A number studies have indicated that employers are more likely to retain older workers than to recruit them (McNair, Flynn and Dutton, 2007; Daniel and Haywood, 2007; Conen, Henkens and Schippers, forthcoming). Yet, not much is known about the factors that affect managers' decisions to re-employ early retirees. The current study aims to fill this void. The main research question addressed is: What factors influence managers' decisions concerning the re-employment of early retirees?

Recent research conducted among employers and employees has shown that stereotypes against older workers are widespread (Van Dalen, Henkens and Schippers, 2010b). Many studies demonstrate that employers often see older workers as inflexible and unwilling (or unable) to adapt to the changing work environment, less productive and more expensive than their

[1] This chapter was published as: K. Karpinska, K. Henkens and J.J. Schippers (2011), The recruitment of early retirees: A vignette study of the factors that affect managers' decisions. *Ageing & Society*, Vol. 31, No. 4, pp. 570-589.

younger colleagues (Chiu *et al.,* 2001; Finkelstein and Burke, 1998; Lee and Clemons, 1985; Loretto, Duncan and White, 2000; Taylor and Walker, 1998a). Moreover, McCann and Gilles (2002) suggested that in many organisations the belief prevails that older workers want to retire as soon as possible. However, the same studies that present negative features of older workers also indicate that older workers are valued for their trustworthiness, specific knowledge and interpersonal skills (Chiu *et al.,* 2001; Finkelstein and Burke, 1998; Lee and Clemons, 1985; Taylor and Walker, 1998a).

While older workers can still be of value to organisations, there is evidence that many older unemployed workers and early retirees who re-enter the workforce take up jobs in the secondary labour market: They find jobs of a lower status than held previously and are engaged for fewer hours (Jorgensen and Taylor, 2008; Taylor and Walker, 1998b). It is not clear to what extent these outcomes reflect the preferences of retirees or are conditioned by employers. There is evidence from the United Kingdom that older workers prefer part-time over full-time jobs (Smeaton, Vegeris and Sahin-Dikmen, 2010; Vickerstaff *et al.,* 2008), but it has also been suggested that older workers who work part time do so not as a result of free choice but rather because they lack opportunities to work full time; many older workers indicate that they wish to increase their labour market participation and work more (Taylor, 2008).

Moreover, a recent study in The Netherlands shows that a substantial number of early retirees re-enter the workforce after retirement, yet others failed to regain employment, even though they express a wish to re-enter the labour force (Henkens, Van Dalen and Van Solinge, 2009). This raises the question: What restrictions do (early) retirees face on the labour market? And what characteristics enhance and limit the employability of early retires? As the impairment of re-entry of retirees into the workforce becomes even more important (due to future labour-force shortages) the potential necessity of retirees to re-entry the labour force requires more insight into the process of their re-employment.

The study was carried out in the Netherlands, where labour market policies have recently changed substantially, from encouragement of early exit (supported by financially attractive early retirement programmes) to encouragement of working longer. The Netherlands is, however, still characterised by a strong early exit culture and low job mobility among older workers (Organisation for Economic Co-operation and Development, 2006). Age discrimination is one of the forces that are assumed to be behind these phenomena. A substantial number of retirees that retired before the mandatory retirement age of 65 years consider their transition into retirement as involuntary (Van Solinge and Henkens, 2007). Although the government has introduced specific macro-level regulations to combat age discrimination, Koppes *et al.* (2009) showed that in the Netherlands age discrimination is still perceived to be substantial: The self-reported rate of age discrimination among older (55-64 years) workers' is 20 percent. In recent years, attempts have been made to increase the labour market participation of older workers. Early-exit schemes have been tightened and the re-entry of (early) retirees is, in most cases, not restricted by labour force regulations or law (*i.e.* employers can hire older worker even after the age of 65). Moreover, various tax policies have been launched: Employers can receive a contribution to the sickness allowances for older workers as well as tax reduction if they hire older workers (aged 50 or more years) or retain older workers already employed (aged 62 or more years) (for more details see Euwals, De Mooij and Van Vuuren, 2009). These policies were intended to simulate labour market participation of older workers. It is yet to be seen, however, whether employers' decisions align with the revised macro-level policies.

The current analysis focuses on how different characteristics of retirees and organisations affect the likelihood of re-employment of a given retiree. To investigate specific employment decisions, a factorial study was designed. This method allows the exploration of actions in context and clarifies people's judgments (Rossi and Anderson, 1982). Factorial design offers an opportunity to simulate employment decisions regarding early retirees. More specifically, we examined virtual hiring decisions of Dutch managers and business students. This extends previous work in the field of employment decisions towards older workers where students were the primary respondents (*e.g.* Avolio and Barret, 1987). Students may have theoretical knowledge and familiarity with the issues under discussion but have no or limited practical experience. Our focus on students *and* managers allowed us to explore the differences between them in how they perceived older workers and in the ways in which they evaluated early retirees.

The remainder of this article is organised as follows: The next section presents the theoretical background and introduces the hypotheses tested, and the section following discusses the methods of data collection and the study design. The results of the analysis are then discussed and finally the conclusions are presented.

2.2.   The determinants of hiring desirability

A basic tenet of organisational theory is that organisations are goal-oriented systems that strive towards profit maximisation, continuity and maintaining a healthy market position (Kalleberg *et al.,* 1996). Managers in organisations are supposed to contribute towards these goals by realising high production levels and low costs, reduced absenteeism and good social relations and by nurturing good sources of knowledge and contacts. Similarly, the achievement of organisational goals depends on the recruitment of qualified staff (Kalleberg *et al.,* 1996). Managers are expected to react to organisation workforce shortages by choosing the best candidates from the applicants. In the selection process, the costs and benefits of hiring different people are evaluated. Managers take these decisions under uncertainty, as individual productivity capabilities are not known at the time an employer hires an applicant (Phelps, 1972; Spence, 1973). Moreover, because workers often change positions over their life course, it is difficult to assess the productivity in and skills for different occupations. Managers deal with this uncertainty by evaluating a combination of observable attributes (Phelps, 1972; Spence, 1973). Successful applicants are thus the ones who are believed to be the most capable of fulfilling the assigned tasks. The same mechanism applies to the employment of early retirees. A manager decides to hire an early retiree if he or she is expected to contribute best towards achieving the organisation's goals.

The decision regarding the hiring of retirees is generally taken by a manager or supervisor, but is always embedded in the broader context of a dynamically changing organisation. Macro-level developments (*e.g.* economic changes and labour-force shortages) influence the managers' choices. When organisations shed jobs during an economic downturn, managers are assumed to assign less priority to hiring retired workers. Hiring retirees has been seen as hampering the work prospects of younger generations and in conflict with norms of generational employment equity. On the other hand, managers facing structural or incidental labour-force shortages may be inclined to hire retirees as a remedy. Therefore we expect that *managers are more inclined to hire early retirees when the organisation faces labour-force shortages.*

Moreover, organisations that face incidental labour-force shortages may require short-term or project-based support. In such situations, staff that accept on-call arrangements, *i.e.* are called into work only as needed (DiNatale, 2001), are required or preferred. There is some evidence that employers are prone to offer older workers part-time, flexible positions

(Taylor, 2008). On-call arrangements are attractive to organisations because they enable erratic staffing needs to be met without the commitment of permanent employment. Consequently, we expect that *managers are more likely to hire retirees who accept on-call contracts.*

Hiring decisions also involve the evaluation of an applicant's various attributes. Human capital is one of the most important features considered at the time. In line with human capital theory (Becker, 1975), investments in human capital are mostly during a person's education, although the skills and experience that accumulate over a long working career have a strong influence on the individual's productivity in different roles (Thurow, 1975; Van Eijs and Heijke, 2000). This job-specific experience is an important facet in managers' selections. Thurow (1975) found that managers take into account potential training cost differences and favour candidates who require less training. The costs of hiring a retiree whose skills and experience are in alignment with the job requirements are significantly lower than those without the matching skills. Consequently, we expect that *managers are more likely to hire retirees who apply for a position that is similar to their previous occupation.*

Human capital accumulated during one's educational and professional career is an important indicator of an early retiree's potential productivity. Further 'investment' in human capital can build it up, but if it ceases deterioration is likely. As indicated by Blanchard and Summers (1986), unemployed workers lose the opportunity to maintain and update their skills. By the same token, the human capital of an early retiree may becomes more and more obsolete the longer they are out of the workforce. Various studies show that employers perceive obsolete skills to go hand-in-hand with lower productivity (Taylor and Walker, 1994; Remery *et al.*, 2003). This, in turn, may result in less support for hiring an early retiree. Therefore we expect that *managers are less inclined to hire early retirees who are absent from the labour force for a long period.*

The health of an older worker is regarded as an important predictor of retention, and we assume that when evaluating the desirability of hiring an early retiree, managers consider the applicant's health condition. Poor health puts the productivity of the worker at risk and cast doubts about performance continuity. Although research shows that older people are less often absent due to sickness, once ill, they need more time to recover (Gellatly, 1995; McCann and Gilles, 2002). Also, their illness is likely to be more severe and consequently the length of absenteeism is higher. As a result, managers may be reluctant to hire retirees whose health condition casts uncertainty about performance continuity. We expect therefore that *managers are more inclined to hire early retirees who are in good health.*

A not necessarily related characteristic is the age of an early retiree. Although age discrimination is prohibited in The Netherlands, it is well established in the literature that there are negative stereotypes about 'older workers'. They are deemed to suffer more often from health deterioration, and thought to be less productive and less willing to be trained (Chui *et al.*, 2001; Finkelstein, Burke and Raju, 1995; Finkelstein and Burke, 1998; Hassel and Perrewe, 1995; Henkens, 2005; Taylor and Walker, 1994; 1998a; Warr and Pennington, 1993). While only a few studies have examined the different stereotypes held about workers aged in the fifties as compared to the early sixties (McGregor and Gray, 2002), we assume that negative stereotypes are associated with greater age. Therefore we expect that *managers are more inclined to hire younger early retirees.*

The last element taken into consideration as a predictor of the propensity to hire a retired worker is the disposition of the retiree to re-enter the workforce. The motivation to return to an occupational career, demonstrated by sending an unsolicited application, might be an indication of the retiree's employability and self management (Fugate, Kinicki and Ashforth, 2004). This proactive attitude in search of a position that matches the applicants' preferences and skills contradicts the stereotypical image of an older person as being inactive (Chiu *et al.*, 2001; Taylor and Walker, 1998a; Loretto and White, 2006; Berger, 2009). This, in turn, may positively influence a manager's attitude towards the hiring of an early retiree. Consequently, we expect that *managers are more likely to hire retirees who send an unsolicited application.*

2.3. Methods

To answer the research question that we have posed, a vignette study was administered to both managers and business students. A vignette study (factorial survey) is a method intended for the investigation of human actions (Ganong and Coleman, 2006; Wallander, 2009). The basic item of the survey is a vignette – a card with a short description of a situation or a person, generated by combining characteristics randomly manipulated by the researcher (Ganong and Coleman, 2006). An important requirement is that the number of characteristics is restricted because participants typically are unable to process large amounts of information. If too many dimensions are introduced, it becomes difficult for the participant to visualise the hypothetical person and the situation clearly (Rossi and Anderson, 1982). In our study, hypothetical retired job applicants were described by several individual characteristics and the hiring decision was placed in a specific organisational context. Each participant was presented with a set of unique vignettes and asked to make hiring decisions regarding the various hypothetical applicants. By randomly varying the characteristics of the virtual applicant, it is possible to determine the weight that respondents attach to each.

2.3.1.   The participants
The survey among managers and students was conducted in 2009. First, a vignette survey was administered to eight managers who attended a focus group meeting on the re-employment of older workers held in May 2009 at the Netherlands Interdisciplinary Demographic Institute (NIDI) (for details see Van Dalen et al., 2009). Conducting vignette experiments during a focus group meeting is common practice (Beaulieu et al., 1999). To increase the number of raters and the potential generalisability of the findings, managers from both public and private organisations were approached using snowball sampling techniques. Snowball sampling has proved to be a valuable method of data collection for groups that are difficult to reach (Salganik and Heckathorn, 2004), as is often the case with managers. In total, 20 managers (12 males, 8 females, mean age 42 years) took part in the study. The managers worked in different employment sectors: Education (2), services (3), public administration (5), health services (2), construction (3), retail (2), and information and communication (3). All of the managers come from the *Randstad* (a conurbation in the south-west of the Netherlands which is the country's commercial and economic hub: It includes the four largest Dutch cities).

In April 2009, the survey was also administered to business students of Utrecht University. In total, 17 students participated in the study (11 males, 6 females, mean age 21 years). In the field of personnel psychology, students are often used as respondents (Sears, 1986). Although they may lack hands-on experience, business students take courses on personnel management, which prepares them for the role of manager. Furthermore, current business students have been confronted with the problems of an ageing society and prospects of their own extended work careers. Both education and generational experience may influence their judgment regarding the hiring of early retirees. In the current study we intend to compare how students view hiring practices relative to supervisors.

2.3.2.   Study design
The vignette study examined the factors that affect managers' and students' decisions to hire virtual early retirees. The instruction was:

Current general labour force shortages mean that there may be limited opportunities for recruiting new workers. Below are various descriptions of early retirees who would like to work for your organisation. Please indicate for each profile, what is the likelihood that you would be willing to hire this person?

The independent variables used in the construction of the vignettes were: *organisational context* (*e.g.* organisation is facing: Structural labour-force shortage, incidental labour-force shortage, no labour-force shortage, need for downsizing); *willingness to accept an on-call appointment* (yes/no); *experience in a similar position* (yes/no); *length of retirement* (retired one month ago, half-a-year ago, or one-and-a-half years ago); *health condition* (healthy/not very healthy); *applicant's age* (58, 62 or 65 years-old); and, *whether a retiree has sent an unsolicited application* (yes/no) (see *table 2.1* for an overview). Given the seven dimensions and their variable number of categories, the possible number of unique combinations or vignettes (the vignette universe) was 576 (*i.e.* $4 \times 2 \times 2 \times 3 \times 2 \times 3 \times 2$). Contrary to a factorial design in which all possible combinations are evaluated, in a vignette survey only a random selection from the vignette universe is judged by respondents (Wallander, 2009). This makes it possible to include a larger number of vignette dimensions and levels in the design, thereby enhancing the resemblance between the real and experimental worlds (Wallander, 2009). In our study, each participant received a random sample of 12 vignettes and rated items on 11-point scales, ranging from '1' (hiring very undesirable/ *Analysis* low priority) to '11' (hiring very desirable/high priority). For an example of a vignette, see *figure 2.1*.

In a vignette design, the unit of analysis is the vignette (Ganong and Coleman, 2006). The total number of observations in this study is 240 for the managers' sample and 204 for the students' sample. We used ordinary least-squares multivariate linear regression analysis to determine which characteristics played a role in the respondents' assessments of the desirability of hiring the virtual older retirees. In order to control for a design effect, we adjusted for clustering at the participant level. We applied robust regression analysis, using the SURVEY command in STATA (Stata, 2003). Without controlling for design effects, we would be likely to produce standard errors that are much smaller than they should be. To test for group differences between the

Table 2.1. The organisational contexts and job applicant's characteristics
in the vignette

Variable	Category
Organisational context	Structural labour-force shortage
	One-time labour-force shortage
	No labour-force shortage
	Need of downsizing
Applicant's characteristics:	
Age	58 years old
	62 years old
	65 years old
Experience in similar position	Yes
	No
Willing to accept a flexible appointment	Yes
	No
Sent an unsolicited application	Yes
	No
Health	Healthy
	Not very healthy
Retired	A month ago
	Half a year ago
	One and a half years ago

managers and students, we used a Chow test of equality between coefficients (Gould, 2002). All independent variables used in the analysis were coded as dummy variables. Variables that originally contained three or four categories (*e.g. organisational context, age of early retirees and length of retirement*) were also transformed into dummy variables representing each category and were included in the analysis with one category serving as a reference category. The dichotomous coding of each level of each predictor through means the magnitude of each observed slope provides meaningful information as to the magnitude of the respondents' ratings. Consequently, the weights estimated for each factor included in the analysis are comparable to one another. This applies not only to comparisons between the different characteristics (*e.g.* the weights assigned by the managers to experience

Figure 2.1. An example vignette

Vignette 5

Current general labour force shortages mean that there may be limited opportunities for recruiting new workers. Below are various descriptions of early retirees who would like to work for your organisation. Please indicate for each profile, what is the likelihood that you would be willing to hire this person?

Situation:

Organisational context	Structural labour-force shortage

Applicant:

Age	58 years-old
Experience in similar position	Yes
Willing to take a flexible appointment	Yes
Sent an unsolicited application	Yes
Health	Healthy
When retired	A month ago

What is the likelihood that you would be willing to hire this person?

1	2	3	4	5	6	7	8	9	10	11
Hiring very undesirable					Neutral			Hiring very desirable		

and to health), but also to the comparisons between managers and business students (*i.e.* whether managers and business students rated characteristics differently).

2.4. The findings

Table 2.2 presents the results. The first column shows the results of the managers' sample and the second column those of the students' sample. The impact of the organisational context on the hiring decisions of managers was in line with our expectations. Both managers and students were more inclined to hire early retirees if an organisation faced structural labour-force shortages, as compared to the reference category (organisation needed to shed jobs). The desirability of hiring was less pronounced in organisations that faced incidental labour-force shortages but was still positive and significant as compared to the reference category. The context of institutions that faced no labour-force shortages or that needed to shed labour did not affect the managers' and students' decisions significantly. In other words, the hiring of older retirees was most likely to occur when an organisation faced structural or, to a lesser extent, incidental labour shortages.

With respect to the retirees' willingness to accept on-call contracts, a discrepancy was evident between the managers' and students' evaluations. Whether a retiree was willing to accept an on-call contract did not affect a manager's decision-making process significantly. Students were more inclined, however, to hire retirees who were willing to work to a more flexible scheme. The applicants' human capital was of great importance for the retirees' chances for re-employment. The managers were more inclined to recruit early retirees who had experience in a similar position to that applied for. Among students, also, the experience of the retiree played an important role in their assessment of the desirability of hiring.

While accumulated human capital increased the managers' disposition to re-employ, its potential decline –as indicated by longer absence from the labour force– diminished hiring desirability. Managers' propensity to hire retirees was not affected by a retiree's absence of half-a-year as compared to one month, but the managers were much less likely to hire somebody who had been unemployed for more than one-and-a-half years (as compared to the reference category). A similar pattern held for the student sample. With regard to early retirees' health condition, the managers were more inclined to hire early retirees with good health. A similar pattern held for students. In fact, health condition was found to be the most important influence on the hiring decisions of the business students.

We also investigated how the age of the early retirees affected managers' and students' willingness to recommend re-employment. In line with our hypothesis, higher age negatively related to managers' and students' willingness to hire early retirees. Managers were much less inclined to hire a retiree aged 62 years than one aged 58 years (the reference category). Retirees at the age of 65 obtained the lowest score, in both managers' and students' samples. While this pattern was similar from both samples, the respective scores show that managers were more negative about hiring the oldest early retirees. The last aspect considered was the perceived disposition of retirees to re-enter the workforce. The results confirm the hypothesis: both managers and students were more inclined to hire an early retiree who had sent an unsolicited application. Although all vignettes presented profiles of applicants motivated to return to the labour force, the raters were more likely

Table 2.2. Multivariate regression of the impact of organisational and individual characteristics on the change of hiring early retirees

	Managers		Business students		
	B	t	B	t	Diff[c]
Constant	2.24***	6.68	2.85***	8.72	
Organisation context					
Structural labour-force shortage	1.88***	5.48	1.53***	4.14	ns
Incidental labour-force shortage	1.30**	2.77	1.44**	3.06	ns
No labour-force shortage	0.06	0.21	0.72	1.85	ns
Need for downsizing (Ref)	—		—		
Applicants characteristics					
Flexible appointment[a]	0.23	0.92	0.75**	3.23	ns
Experience in similar position[a]	1.76***	5.18	1.17***	5.5	ns
Retired					
A month ago (Ref.)	—		—		
Half a year ago	-0.21	-0.75	-0.33	-1.51	ns
One and a half years ago	-0.80**	-3.10	-0.47*	-2.32	ns
Healthy[b]	0.56**	2.01	1.59***	10.93	**
Age					
58 years old (Ref.)	—		—		
62 years old	-0.71**	-2.76	-0.67**	-2.43	ns
65 years old	-1.54***	-6.71	-0.95***	-4.77	ns
Sent unsolicited application[a]	0.59*	2.16	0.62**	3.33	ns
	0.41		0.45		
R-squared					
Sample size	240		204		

Notes: Ref.: reference category. [a] yes=1; no=0. [b] 1=healthy; 0=not very healthy. [c] Difference between coefficients.
Significance levels: *p<0.05; **p<0.01; ***p<0.001.

to select those who took additional action to gain employment. In other words, this extra activity on the part of early retirees 'paid off'.

2.4.1.   Hiring desirability
To gauge the priorities that managers assigned when deciding whether to hire early retirees, the 'hiring desirability' scores for different groups of applicants were calculated. Based on the employability of applicants (*e.g.* capability of a person to gain employment, maintain it or obtain new employment; Fugate, Kinicki and Ashforth, 2004), we distinguished three categories: 'high', 'moderate' and 'low' employability. A retiree with *high employability* was indentified as an applicant who had experience in a similar position, retired a month ago, was healthy, 58-years-old, and had sent an unsolicited application. *Moderate employability* referred to an applicant who had experience in a similar position, retired no more than half-a-year ago, was healthy, 62-years-old, and had sent an unsolicited application. *Low employability* described an applicant who did not have experience in a similar position, retired at least one-and-a-half years ago, was healthy, 65-years-old, and had sent an unsolicited application. The scores for each category of retirees were computed and are presented in *table 2.3*.

In general, the hiring of retirees was a low priority for the managers. Even in the most beneficial conditions, if we consider a retiree with all characteristics in favour of re-employment (*e.g.* highly employable; see figure 2.1 for an example), in an organisation facing structural labour-force shortages, the overall score was 6.6 on a scale from 1 to 11. This score has almost a neutral value. For each retiree whose profile differs, the scores representing the desirability for hiring fell, being the lowest for the applicants with low employability, indicating that re-entry becomes undesirable or very undesirable. We also observed that virtually identical scores were assigned to respective categories of applicants in organisations facing *no labour-force shortages and needed to downsize*.

2.4.2.   Differences between managers and students
The results of the vignette study show that when making decisions about the desirability of hiring of retirees, managers and business students evaluated similar factors in the same way but with some differences in weights. The questions that we address here is whether business students differed significantly from managers in their assessments, and the extent to which there were significant differences among the various vignette characteristics. To answer these questions, we examined whether the regression coefficients for the various characteristics significantly differed using the Chow test

Table 2.3. Hiring desirability of different categories of early retirees —
managers' scores

	Applicant's employability		
Organisation	High	Moderate	Low
Structural labour-force shortages	6.6	6.0	3.0
Incidental labour-force shortages	6.5	5.5	2.4
No labour-force shortages	5.2	4.3	1.1
Need for downsizing	5.3	4.5	1.0

(Gould, 2002). Interestingly, managers did not attach as much importance to the health status of retired applicants as business students (managers B = 0.56, students B = 1.59, F (degrees of freedom 1, 420) = 11.19, p<0.001). In fact, the retiree's heath condition was the most important factor affecting students' evaluations of hiring desirability. Other factors related to individual and organisational attributes did not differ significantly, indicating that fairly consistent weights were assigned to these factors by managers and business students.

2.5. Discussion and conclusions

This study has investigated the factors that affect decisions to recruit early retirees. The research question was: what are the factors influencing managers' decisions of re-employment of early retirees? A vignette survey was used to collect data on the hiring decisions of managers and business students. In the vignette survey, profiles of hypothetical retirees were presented to the participants who accordingly made recruitment decisions. The analysis focused on the impact of organisational labour-force shortages and various characteristics of potential applicants on managers' propensity to hire early retirees. Multivariate regression tools for clustered data were applied to analyse the data and the weights assigned to each factor were assessed.

It has been shown that managers' employment hiring decisions about early retirees are affected by the organisational context. Managers in organisations facing structural or incidental labour-force shortages are more inclined to hire early retirees, while this issue is irrelevant in other organisations. The results suggest that re-employment comes into the picture only when organisations have recruitment problems. This finding corroborates earlier evidence. Remery *et al.* (2003) suggested that although Dutch managers do not actively recruit older workers, a significant share would consider doing so in the case of labour-force shortages, because other sources can quickly 'run dry'. Our results imply that while labour-force shortages may be beneficial to early retirees' employment prospects, their chances for re-employment are low when labour force supply is sufficient and positions could be filled by younger applicants.

Considering the individual characteristics of applicants, we found that experience in a position similar to the one applied for increases the retiree's chances of re-employment. While this aspect contributed significantly to managers' approval, there is another side to the coin: If managers highly value specific forms of human capital, they may be less willing to employ retirees without the endowment. This suggests that the opportunity structure available for retirees is contingent on earlier work experience and, moreover, that access to other occupations is limited. With respect to the age of retirees, our study clearly shows that despite anti-discrimination policies, managers are still greatly influenced by age. The managers were much less inclined to employ older than younger early retirees. This finding puts into perspective employees' and job applicants' complaints about age discrimination. As shown by Koppes *et al.* (2009), older workers often indicate they are subjected to age-related discrimination, and Berger (2009) found that applicants perceive age discrimination in selection processes. Our results suggest that such complaints may reflect actual hiring practice, and that recruitment has not yet implemented anti-discriminatory public policies.

The influence of perceived attitudes of retirees towards re-employment –represented by sending an unsolicited application– was also found substantial. As illustrated in a recent study by Henkens, Van Solinge and Cozijnsen (2009), a worker's perceived motivation to retire was an important weight in managers' decisions of whether to retain them (or to advise early retirement). In a similar vein, Sterns and Kaplan (2003) emphasised the importance of skills maintenance for the employment success of older workers. The prominence of retirees' self management is also evident in our findings, because it swayed managers to consider hiring retirees. This result suggests that managers value applicants whose appearance may promise continuing employability. Moreover, this result implies a more active role of retirees in the re-employment process; their employment chances may be more influenced by their own circumstances than the managers' preconceptions or structural constraints. Also, the managers' and students' decisions regarding early retirees clearly show the importance of employment continuity. The results suggest that only a short absence is permitted; longer episodes of unemployment are punished. This implies that early retirees who are not able to regain employment soon after retirement are at risk of a permanent and involuntary exclusion from the labour force.

Another issue addressed in the paper is the differences between the managers and the business students in their assessments of the desirability of hiring early retirees. We found that they differed primarily with respect to the weight they assigned to an applicant's health, for on no other factor did a significant difference emerge. For the students, health condition was the most important influence on their judgment. Most were probably young and healthy, which may have predisposed them to see good health as a prerequisite for employment.

We conclude with some methodological remarks. As is true of studies conducted in laboratory settings, one advantage of a factorial survey is that the researcher controls the various levels of the independent variables. Factorial surveys are therefore very suitable for investigations of issues that are normally difficult to examine because they are rare events or involve complex multi-attribute situations. A clear advantage of this method is that a relatively small number of respondents create a large data set by which to analyse a complex decision making process (Ganong and Coleman, 2006; Wallander, 2009). The method also has disadvantages, however, with the major limitation being that the respondents assess a hypothetical situation. The participants may act or decide in ways that would be different in a real-life situation. Another limitation of our application of the method was the relatively few participants, which did not allow the incorporation of either their characteristics (*e.g.* gender and age) or those of the companies. Combining a large scale survey and a vignette study would increase the possibility of disentangling the different aspects of the process described. This design, with a considerably larger sample of the managers, would permit the application of multilevel modelling and consequently answer the research questions more adequately. Also, our study did not allow a more comprehensive exploration of managers' attitudes towards different facets of flexible working arrangements (*e.g.* part-time versus full-time or permanent versus temporary posts). Clearly, these issues deserve more attention in future research.

Moreover, our study did not take the gender of the early retiree into account, due to the country specific reasons. The employment of older women is rather limited in the Netherlands, and so few women can or intend *to return* to the labour force. The predominant picture in the Dutch context is thus the one of the male early retiree. We recognise, however, that with current changes in the labour market and the increasing participation of women, future research will need to examine gender-related differences in hiring practices (Lorreto and Duncan, 2004).

The findings show that early retirees are not received with open arms by employing organisations; in the best case, managers are moderately positive about hiring them, but overall the likelihood of hiring early retirees is relatively low. This is an important observation in view of the changing dynamics of retirement in the Netherlands. As indicated before, labour-market exits are changing, but which new trajectories and patterns become available depend largely on employers' and managers' support. Our study demonstrates that managers are hindering the dynamics of change by restricting the re-employment of people who are around the retirement age.

3. Hiring retirees. Impact of age norms and stereotypes[1]

3.1. Introduction

Changes in the population structure and the ageing workforce suggest that employers may need to retain and hire more older workers (Elster, 1989). Bridge employment, *i.e.* employment that occurs between career jobs and permanent retirement (Wang and Shultz, 2010) is expected to help close the gap in labour force supply that will occur along with the retirement of the baby-boomers (Wang *et al.*, 2008). As retirement has come to be seen as a more dynamic and gradual transition from a working to a non-working life, a growing number of older workers may opt for bridge employment in the future.

Much research in the field of bridge employment has focused on older workers and their motivation, preferences and ability to extend their working career (Weckerle and Shultz, 1999; Jones and McIntosh, 2010) *i.e.*, on the supply side. Those studies indicate that individual attributes like age and good health, along with attractive working conditions (such as challenging work) promote older workers' intentions of continued employment (Kim and Feldman, 2000; Wang *et al.*, 2008). Growing evidence suggests that the share of workers willing to extend their working career is increasing (Von Bonsdorff *et al.*, 2009).

While older workers have some agency about whether to retire from work or to enter self-employment (Bruce *et al.*, 2000), prospects of returning to the labour force for early retirees (*i.e.*, individuals who exit the work force before the mandatory retirement age) are largely determined by employers and the availability of jobs in organisations (Munnell and Sass, 2008). Although managers are the ones deciding on the hiring, the demand side for older workers has not yet attracted much attention.

Karpinska and colleagues show that the hiring propensity of early retirees is low, also for those who are expected to have a high employability (Karpinska *et al.*, 2011). This raises the question whether the hiring of early retirees is influenced not only by their individual attributes but also by managers' dispositional attitudes towards older workers. Although early retirees are a subcategory of older workers they are likely to be similarly affected by ageist

---

[1] Will appear as: Karpinska, K., K. Henkens and J. Schippers (forthcoming), Hiring retirees. Impact of age norms and stereotypes. *Journal of Managerial Psychology.*

attitudes. Our study integrates these aspects of labour market participation of older workers and asks: *How do ageist stereotypes and age norms, next to attributes of applicants, affect managers' propensity to hire early retirees?*

There is a wide body of literature that focuses on the general attitudes of employers. Those attitudes frame managers' perceptions of older workers and their abilities (Van Dalen *et al.*, 2010b), and can take the form of age norms and stereotypes. The concept of social norms and their impact on behaviour has been one of the paradigms of sociology for decades and has been gaining recognition in economics (Elster, 1989; Coleman, 1990). Norms as rules of behaviour coordinate interactions with others and are believed to guide individuals in social situations. Stereotypes form important cognitive tools that facilitate the processing of complex information (Hilton and Von Hippel, 1996), and as such, influence behavioural response (Bargh *et al.*,1996).

Although it has been suggested that both stereotypes and age norms may affect employers' behaviour (Chiu *et al.*, 2001; Finkelstein and Burke, 1998; Lee and Clemons, 1985; Loretto *et al.*, 2000) not much empirical evidence has been presented to support this connection. Studies on age norms in employment transitions often describe organisational age norms and factors behind them (Settersten and Hagestad, 1996; Settersten, 1998; Lawrence, 1996). Specific managerial norms and their impact on behaviour have been neglected. Similarly, while there are few studies analysing the effect of age stereotypes on attitudes towards different aspects of employment of older workers (Chiu *et al.*, 2001; Henkens, 2005; Hassell and Perrewe, 1995), they do not focus on their impact on decisions. A number of studies used an experimental design to evaluate decisions regarding older workers (in basket or audit experiments; see Bendick *et al.*, 1997; Finkelstein *et al.*, 1995). Yet, not many have combined those two paths to assess the possible impact of general attitudes on individual employment decisions.

Our study contributes to the existing literature in two ways. Firstly, combining information on the demand and supply side helps disentangle complex aspects of the hiring process. As suggested by Posthuma and Campion (2009) most studies that investigate ageist stereotypes and labour market outcomes focus on one dimension only, neglecting the organisational context. In the current work we not only estimate the effect of general attitudes (age norms and stereotypes) on hiring behaviour regarding early retirees but simultaneously we also evaluate applicants' attributes and the effect of organisational forces. In addition, we estimate the effect of both age norms and age stereotypes on a specific decision. Liefbroer and Billari (2010) argue that although impact of age norms on human behaviour has been debated for decades now, it is still lacking an extensive empirical test. We contribute to this debate by offering an empirical test of the possible impact of general attitudes on managers' (hypothetical) hiring behaviour.

To investigate this specific employment decision, a combination of a survey and a vignette study was designed. The data for our study were collected in two stages. First we carried out the survey among managers and collected information on age norms and age-related stereotypes (Study 1). During Study 2, which took place a month later, a vignette study among the same group of managers was conducted. A factorial design is a method that allows the exploration of actions in context and offers an opportunity to simulate employment decisions (Rossi and Anderson, 1982). All managers were asked to make hiring decisions for five hypothetical applicants.

The study was carried out in the Netherlands, where labour market policies have recently changed substantially, from encouragement of early exit (supported by financially attractive early retirement programmes) to encouragement of working longer (Van Dalen and Henkens, 2002). A recent policy change assumes extending working lives until the age of 67. In 2009 less than 50 percent of workers aged 55-64 was employed (Statistics Netherlands, 2009), and although workers retire later in the Netherlands than they used to, in 2010 only 27 percent of workers retired at the statutory retirement age of 65. Age discrimination is one of the forces that are assumed to be behind this phenomenon. A substantial number of early retirees consider their transition into retirement as involuntary (Van Solinge and Henkens, 2007). Despite policies that aim at combating age discrimination, Koppes *et al.* (2009) showed that in the Netherlands age discrimination is still perceived to be substantial: The self-reported rate of age discrimination among older (55-64 years) workers is 20 percent. Re-entry of (early) retirees is, in most cases, not restricted by labour force regulations or law (*i.e.*, employers can hire older worker even after the age of 65). And although re-entry after early retirement increases, many retirees are unsuccessful in finding a job after retirement even in times when shortages on the labour market are widespread (Van Dalen *et al.*, 2009).

3.2. Theory

Recruitment is a process where the demand for new employees is confronted with the supply of available applicants. The demand for new staff is conditional on the organisational circumstances, and managers operate as a link between the organisational goals and the work environment, as they are directly responsible for recruitment (Kalleberg *et al.*, 1996). There are three types of factors that intertwine in the recruitment process: Organisational characteristics, managers' attributes and applicants' attributes. Below we discuss in detail how each of these aspects affects hiring decisions.

3.2.1.   Organisational context

A basic tenet of organisational theory is that organisations are goal-oriented systems that strive towards profit maximisation, continuity, and maintaining a healthy market position (Kalleberg *et al.*, 1996). Managers in organisations are supposed to contribute to these goals by, among others, recruitment of qualified staff (Kalleberg *et al.*, 1996). Managers are expected to react to organisational workforce shortages by choosing the best candidates from the applicant pool. Successful applicants are thus the ones who are believed to be the most capable of fulfilling the assigned tasks. The same mechanism applies to the employment of early retirees. A manager decides to hire an early retiree if he or she is expected to contribute best towards achieving the organisation's goals.

The decision regarding the hiring of early retirees is generally taken by a manager, but is always embedded in the broader context of a dynamically changing organisation. Macro-level developments (*e.g.* economic changes and labour-force shortages) influence managers' choices. When organisations shed jobs during an economic downturn, managers are assumed to assign less priority to hiring retired workers as it might hamper the work prospects of younger generations and conflict with norms of generational employment equity (Van Dalen and Henkens, 2002). On the other hand, managers facing structural or incidental labour-force shortages may be inclined to hire early retirees as a remedy. Hence we expect managers to be more inclined to hire early retirees when the organisation faces labour-force shortages.

3.2.2.   Attributes of managers

In the selection process, managers evaluate hiring desirability of applicants by assessing their productivity. There is a level of uncertainty in hiring decisions, as individual productivity capabilities are not known at the time of hiring (Phelps, 1972; Spence, 1973). Managers deal with this uncertainty by evaluating a combination of observable attributes of applicants (Phelps, 1972; Spence, 1973). Employers also have access to what Phelps (1972) calls "previous statistical experience": information on how certain categories of employees tend to behave and develop. As productivity assessment is a complex information-processing task, managers apply categorisation and stereotyping as most effective cognitive tools (Van Dalen *et al.*, 2010b). Social norms are also applied in this process. We elaborate on both below.

Age norms
Social norms are customary rules of behaviour that coordinate human interaction. Norms either operate as part of actors' environment or shape individuals' predispositions (Etzioni, 2000). While the first aspect depicts external control of human behaviour with external restriction and sanctions, the latter proposes that norms are internalised and no external sanctions are necessary, as norms determine dispositions and goals (Etzioni, 2000; Horne, 2003).

The current study focused on age norms regarding employment transitions (Settersten and Hagestad, 1996). While age norms about the 'right time' to retire are formally expressed in age boundaries established by public and private pension schemes, the life-course paradigm presumes that the transition from work to retirement is also influenced by informal age-graded norms (Settersten and Hagestad, 1996; Settersten, 1998; Van Solinge and Henkens, 2007). Re-entry to the labour force is a more complex process and norms held by managers can have a substantial impact on its course. We expect that the perception of the normative timetable (the proper age for retirement versus extended employment) affects, next to applicants' attributes, managers' hiring decisions. Support of older applicants' return to the labour market happens when managers believe that this is still appropriate. In the present study we hypothesize that the higher the age norm of managers regarding older workers' participation in the labour market, the more likely they are to hire an early retiree.

Stereotypes about older workers
Stereotypes are the beliefs about characteristics, attributes and behaviours of members of certain groups, based on their personal characteristics (such as age, gender, social status (Hilton and Von Hippel, 1996). People make use of those categorisations as they are assumed to be cognitively economical. Moreover, they form the basis of an automatic behavioural response (Bargh *et al.*, 1996; Macrae and Bodenhausen, 2001).

While many studies demonstrate that employers often see older workers as inflexible, unwilling (or unable) to adapt to the changing work environment and less productive than their younger colleagues, the same studies confirm that older workers are valued for their trustworthiness, specific knowledge and interpersonal skills (Chiu *et al.*, 2001; Finkelstein and Burke, 1998; Lee and Clemons 1985; Taylor and Walker, 1998a). Van Dalen *et al.* (2010b) have captured this dual aspect of stereotypes regarding older workers' productivity. They showed that employers' attitudes towards older workers reflect two dimensions: Hard and soft skills. Soft skills consist primarily of qualities that play a role in job performance, such as commitment to the organisation, reliability and social skills. Those skills can be characterised as 'organisational citizenship behaviour' – pro-social behaviour that is not job-specific but which is important for the broader organisational environment in which jobs are performed (Van Dalen *et al.*, 2010b; Ng and Feldman, 2008). Hard skills, on the contrary, reflect mental and physical capacity, willingness to learn new skills and adapt to new technologies, and flexibility. Although very different, both types of skills contribute to employees' productivity.

One important aspect of stereotypes is that prevailing views may affect managers' discriminatory attitudes and behaviour. Chiu *et al.* (2001) showed that the more respondents perceive older workers as being able to adapt to change, the more favourable their views are on the training and promotion of older workers. By the same token, less positive attitudes may lead to discriminatory behaviour. Therefore we expect more positive perceptions of older workers' soft and hard skills to lead to a greater propensity of managers to hire early retirees.

3.2.3.   Applicants' attributes
An important aspect of hiring decisions is the evaluation of an applicant's attributes. Four issues are deemed to be important here: Human capital, health condition, flexibility and social capital.

Human capital is a set of skills that is embodied in the ability to perform labour and to produce economic value. As it is a direct measure of productivity, human capital is one of the most important characteristics of applicants evaluated in the employment process. In line with human capital theory (Becker, 1975), individuals' investments in human capital are made during the person's educational career, although the skills and experience that is built up over a long working career have a strong influence on the individual's productivity in different roles (Thurow, 1975; Eijs and Heijke, 2000). Thurow (1975) found that managers take into account potential training cost differences and favour candidates who require less training. The costs of hiring an early retiree, whose skills and experience are in alignment with the job requirements are significantly lower than for those without the matching skills, increasing the likelihood of successful application.

Human capital is an important indicator of an early retiree's potential productivity, yet deterioration is likely if it ceases. As indicated by Blanchard and Summers (1986), unemployed workers lose the opportunity to maintain and update their skills. By the same token, the human capital of early retirees becomes more obsolete with the length of their retirement. Various studies show that employers perceive obsolete skills to go hand-in-hand with lower productivity (Taylor and Walker, 1994; Remery *et al.*, 2003). This, in turn, will result in less support for hiring an early retiree.

Hiring decisions regarding older workers also involve the estimation of the health condition of an older applicant. Poor health puts worker productivity at risk and casts doubts on performance continuity. While older persons are less likely to be absent due to illness, once ill they take more time to recover (Gellatly, 1995; McCann and Giles, 2003). As health status is hardly known during the application process, managers may refer to observable attributes. Energetic physical appearance may serve as a proxy for good health and therefore be the best measure of an applicant's productivity that managers can obtain at the offset of the hiring history. A more energetic appearance can sway managers towards hiring an older worker, as this impression contradicts stereotypical images of older inactive persons with a deteriorated health (Berger, 2009). We therefore predict that the hiring chances of older workers are higher for those applicants who appear energetic.

Another factor that can affect managers' decision is applicants' flexibility. As organisations may require short-term or project-based support, staff that accepts being called into work only as needed (DiNatale, 2001) is preferred, and is thus more likely to be hired. There is some evidence that employers are prone to offer older workers part-time, flexible positions (Taylor, 2008). On-call arrangements in different forms (from fixed hours to part-time employment) are attractive to organisations because they enable dynamic staffing needs to be met without the commitment of permanent employment. Also importantly, applicants' social capital can have an impact on their hiring success. An applicant's access to helpful networks provides information on job openings and can be a source of valuable recommendations. Marsden and Garman (2001) indicate that the use of referrals is one practice applied by employers in the staffing process, as it lowers hiring costs and allows convening rich and trustworthy information. Employers put more trust in the recommendations offered by their contacts, as these contacts act as a guarantee; their reputation is at stake if they provide false or unreliable information (Marsden and Garman, 2001). Hence the hiring chances of early retirees rise with recommendations, especially if the recommending party is a business contact of the manager.

3.2.4. Hypotheses

In the proceeding section we identified three groups of factors important in manager's recruitment decisions. For each group of factors a hypothesis can be formulated. With respect to organisational circumstances, we expect that *managers are more inclined to hire early retirees when organisations face labour force shortages rather than when organisation face no labour force shortages* (Hypothesis 1). For managers' attitudes, two hypotheses can be presented. First, we predict that *managers, who have a higher age norm with respect to retirement, will be more inclined to hire an early retiree* (Hypothesis 2a). Secondly, we predict that *managers who hold more positive view of older workers as compared to younger counterparts will be more likely to hire early retirees* (Hypothesis 2b). Last hypothesis refers to individual characteristics of early retirees. We predict that *early retirees will have higher hiring chances if they have experience in a similar position, are willing to take a flexible appointment and have been absent from the labour market for a shorter period, appear energetic and have a recommendation from the manager's social network* (Hypothesis 3).

In the complexity of real life situations the above mentioned groups of factors will interact with each other. One might assume that an organisational context frames managers' decisions strongly. When organisations are shedding jobs, the impact of negative age norms and stereotypes may be activated more strongly, while in time of shortages in the labour market, their effect may be slumbering and individual characteristics of applicants will be decisive in the recruitment process. Similarly, organisations active in different fields will have different requirements regarding older workers and their employment; as in some sectors human capital will weigh more, in others physical fitness will be of greater importance. Consequently, employment decisions will be affected differently.

3.3. Data and methods

For this study we used a multi-method approach, combining survey research (Study 1) with a factorial study (Study 2). First a survey was administered to managers and one month later the same managers were approached again to complete a vignette study. By introducing a monthly gap between the studies we limited the risk of bias related to potential carryover effects (Leeuw *et al.*, 2008). Moreover, this approach, with a semi-panel design, is well suited to analyse the effect of stereotypes and norms on (hypothetical) behaviour. Liefbroer and Billari (2010) suggested that to properly analyse the effect of norms on behaviour, the perception of norms needs to be observed before the actual behaviour.

The data was collected using the LISS panel (Longitudinal Internet Studies for the Social Sciences of Tilburg University, http://www.lissdata.nl/lissdata/). LISS is an Internet panel that consists of 5.000 households, comprising 8.000 individuals. All individuals were selected based on a true probability sample of households drawn from the population register by Statistics Netherlands.

3.3.1.   Study 1
During Study 1, a battery of questions on stereotypes regarding older workers, age norms, and background characteristics was distributed to LISS respondents who held managerial positions during the time of the study. The data was collected in April 2010.

Participants
Based on the question: *Do you supervise others?*, a total of 700 LISS members (managers) were approached. The response rate for Study 1 was 73.6 percent (N=515). Although the study was aimed at different-level managers in organisations, not all of the respondents satisfied this condition. Further selection based on the question: *What is your current occupation?* eliminated 186 non-managers from the sample. The final sample consisted of 238 managers. Three categories of managers are represented according to the LISS panel distinction:[2] *Higher supervisory positions* (manager, director, owner of large company, supervisory civil servant; N=99), *intermediate supervisory or commercial positions* (head representative, department manager, shopkeeper; N=99) and *supervisory manual workers* (N=40). The sample consisted of 182 males and 56 females and the mean age of respondents was 45.3 (range 24-65, SD=9.45). For details see *table 3.1.*

Measurements
Age norm is based on the open question: *At what age do you consider a person too old to work in your organisation for 20 hours a week or more?* The answers ranged from 40 to 100. To avoid potential problems with outliers, the answers were truncated and ranged from 50 to 80. Mean age was 64.7 years with a SD of 5.9. Modal value of age was 65 —approximately 32 percent of respondents indicated that the retirement age of 65 is when a person is too old to work 20 hours or more. About 9 percent of managers indicated age norms for retirement transition to be in the range between 50-59 years, for

---

[2]   For distinctions between respondents' professions see: http://www.lissdata.nl/dataarchive/study_ units/view/145

60,5 percent of respondents within the range 60-65 years and for roughly 30 percent— above age 65. Also alternative coding of the age norm were tested, but as median and mode values of age norm were not affected by the coding, the original measurement was kept. For the distribution of the answers see *figure 3.1*.

Stereotype variables are based on two questions: *To what extent do the following characteristics apply to workers aged 60 or older?*, and: *To what extent do the following characteristics apply to workers aged 35 and younger?* The characteristics presented in both cases were: *Flexibility, social skills, commitment to organisation, creativity, management skills, reliability, willingness to learn, physical capacity, resistance to stress, new technology skills*. Two factors were selected based on the factor analysis, namely: *Soft* and *hard skills* (Van Dalen *et al.*, 2010b). In the consecutive analyses relative scores scales (level to which those characteristics apply to older workers as compared to their younger counterparts) were computed. The *soft skills* scale consists of the following four items: *Social skills, commitment to organisation, management skills, reliability* (range 1-4; Cronbach's alpha=0.859). The mean value exceeds 1 (M=1.16) implying that workers aged 60 and more were perceived to posses those skills to a greater extent than younger workers. The *hard skills* scale is based on these items: *Creativity, flexibility, willingness to learn, physical capacity, resistance to stress, new technology skills* (range 1-4; Cronbach's alpha=0.839). The *hard skills* scale is lower than 1 (M=0.68) meaning that managers consider those skills as more applicable to workers aged 35 and younger than to older workers.

As both age norms and age-related stereotypes reflect managers' attitudes towards older workers, we assessed their correlation to rule out multicolinearity problems. The results indicate that stereotypes as measured in this study were not strongly correlated with the measure of age norms; the correlation between the soft qualities scale and age norm was 0.157 (p<0.001) and for the hard qualities scale it was 0.126 (p<0.001).

During Study 1 also information on the control variables was collected. We controlled for *job level of subordinates*. Settersen and Hagestad (1996) suggest that age norms may vary not only across different contexts but also across occupations. This variable was based on managers' answers to the open question: *What is the occupation that you supervise most frequently?* We constructed three variables representing occupations. In the first step all occupations were coded according to the occupational codes of Statistics

Table 3.1. Descriptive statistics, N=238

	Min	Max	Mean/%	St. Dev.
Dependent variable				
Hiring chances	1	11	4.15	0.06
Independent variables				
Stereotypes				
Hard qualities	1	4	0.68	0.27
Soft qualities	1	4	1.16	0.41
Age norm	50	80	64.5	6.04
Characteristics of respondents				
Managerial position				
Higher supervisory positions	0	1	41.5	
Intermediate supervisory or commercial positions	0	1	41.5	
Supervisory manual workers	0	1	16.8	
Age (years)	24	65	45.3	9.4
Gender (male- reference category)	0	1	76.4	
Education (years)	8	18	15.5	2.55
Job level of subordinates				
Manual	0	1	19.7	
Intermediary administrative	0	1	47.8	
Professional	0	1	32.2	
Size of organisation	10	10,000	375.8	1,048.54
Sector				
Industry	0	1	26.4	
Services	0	1	38.8	
Public	0	1	34.8	

Source: LISS panel study.

Netherlands[3], arriving at five categories of occupations which were then limited to three categories: *Professional occupations* (for which higher education was required), *administrative positions* and *manual occupations*. Details regarding the coding are available upon request.

Other control variables were *respondents' gender* and *respondents' age*. *Sector* of the organisation was based on the question: *In which sector is your company operating?* Following the European Commission division

---

[3] Standaard Beroepenclassificatie 2010, http://www.cbs.nl/NR/rdonlyres/6221F84D-BEDD-4B0C-B9ED-ADF076E4D769/0/2010sbcclassificatieschema.pdf

Figure 3.1. The distribution of the age norm among managers in the LISS sample

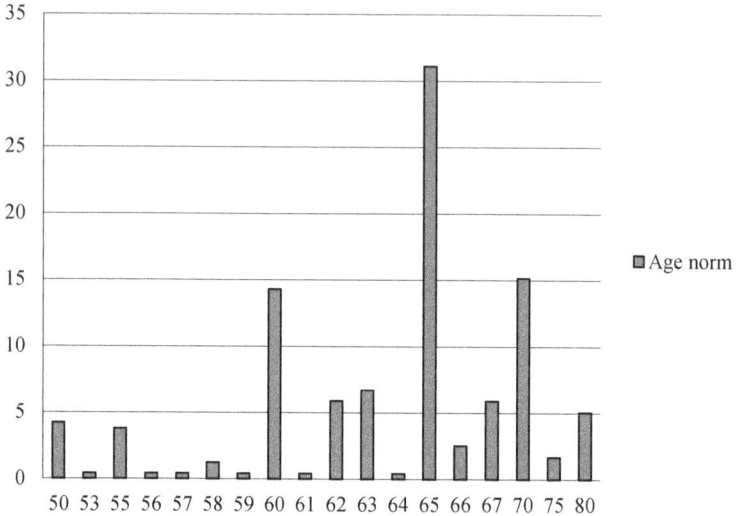

Source: LISS panel study.

of sectors, three categories were constructed: *Industry, services and public.* Comparison with Eurostat statistics (European Commission, 2006) revealed that the data are representative for the sector distribution in the Netherlands.

3.3.2.   Study 2
Study 2 consisted of a vignette survey, which is a method intended for the investigation of human actions. The basic item of the survey is a vignette, which is a short description of a situation or a person, generated by combining characteristics randomly manipulated by the researcher (Ganong and Coleman, 2006; Wallander, 2009).

Participants
For Study 2, all respondents who participated in the first round were contacted and a total of 238 questionnaires filled in completely. The response rate for Study 2 was 82.3 percent. In Study 2 each manager judged 5 vignettes, resulting in a total of 1.190 vignettes.

Measurements
In Study 2 respondents judged vignettes. The eight vignette characteristics were: *organisation characteristics* (facing structural labour force shortages,

incidental labour force shortages, no labour force shortages, need for downsizing); *experience in a similar position* (yes/no); *availability* (full-time only, part-time, fixed hours, flexible appointment), *length of retirement* (applicant retired a month ago, half a year ago, one-and-a-half years ago); *physical appearance* (appears vital/ does not appear vital); *was recommended* (by a business partner, by a colleague or no recommendation). In the vignettes we also included *applicant's age* (58, 62 and 65) and *gender* (male/female). Given all possible combinations of the variables and their respective levels, the universe of 3.456 unique vignettes was created (*i.e.* 4x3x2x2x4x3x2x3; for details see *table 3.2*). None of the vignettes contained impossible combination of the factors. All the variables measured in Study 2 were included in the analysis as dummy variables, so the weights estimated for each factor included are comparable.

In contrast with a factorial design in which all possible combinations are evaluated, in a vignette survey only a random selection from the universe of vignettes is judged by respondents (Wallander, 2009). In our study, each participant received a random sample of 5 vignettes (random selection with replacement). Each rater was required to rate each vignette on an 11-point scale, ranging from 1 (hiring very undesirable) to 11 (hiring very desirable). For an example of a vignette used in the study, see *figure 3.2*.

3.3.3.   Analysis
In a vignette design, the unit of analysis is the vignette (Ganong and Coleman, 2006). As each manager judged five vignettes, our factorial survey data have a hierarchical structure by design and consequently, observations are not independent (Wallander, 2009). Multilevel models were applied to deal with the hierarchical structure of the data (Hox, 2002).

In total, four models were estimated. The first model –the 'empty model'– was estimated to decompose the variance between the two levels of analysis: level of applicants (level 1) and managers' level (level 2). In Model 2 we introduced managers' age norms and stereotypes as well as control variables of managers' organisations. Models 3 and 4 introduced attributes that were included in the vignettes. Specifically, Model 3 depicts the effect of organisational labour force shortages, and Model 4 also incorporates applicants' characteristics.

3.4. Results

Table 3.3 presents the results of our analyses. Model 1 contains only fixed and random effects of the intercept. Intraclass correlation shows that this level accounts for 38.3 percent of the total variance in hiring scores. The intercept illustrates that on average the hiring desirability was rather low and took a value of 4.1 (on a scale ranging from 1 to 11).

Model 2 in table 3.3 shows the fixed effects of age norms and stereotypes on hiring decisions. In line with our hypothesis, age norms do affect managers' evaluations of the hiring desirability of early retired applicants. The higher the age limit, the higher the propensity to hire an early retiree. We also tested how different dimensions of age stereotypes affected hiring preferences of the early retirees. Contrary to our expectations, neither soft-skills nor hard-skills stereotypes affected the hiring desirability of early retirees significantly.

Figure 3.2. Example of a vignette

Below are various descriptions of ealy retirees who would like to work for your organisation. Please indicate, for each profile, what is the likelihood of you being willing to hire this person for a position that you most often supervise?

Context:	
Organisational context	Structural labour-force shortage
Applicant:	
Age	65
Gender	Male
Experience in similar position	Yes
Availability	Fixed hours
Last worked	1.5 years ago
Physical appearance	Energetic
Recommende by	A business partner

What is the likelihood that you would be willing to hire this person for a position that you most often supervise?

1	2	3	4	5	6	7	8	9	10	11
Hiring very undesirable					Neutral			Hiring very desirable		

Table 3.2. Characteristics as found in the vignette and the expected effects, including reference categories

Item	Categories	Expected effect on hiring probability
Organisation		
Organisational condition	Structural labour force shortages	+
	Incidental labour force shortages	+
	No labour force shortages	+
	Need for downsizing	Reference category
Applicants		
Age (years)	58	Reference category
	62	-
	65	-
Gender	Male	+
	Female	Reference category
Experience in similar positions	Yes	+
	No	Reference category
Availability	Full-time only	Reference category
	Part-time	+
	Fixed hours	+
	Flexible appointment	+
Last worked	One month ago	Reference category
	Half a year ago	-
	One-and-a-half years ago	-
Physical appearance	Energetic	+
	Not very enegetic	Reference category
Recommended by	A business partner	+
	A colleague	+
	No specific recommendation	Reference category

Source: LISS panel study.

In this model we also controlled for the characteristics of the managers and the context of organisations they are employed in. With respect to organisation characteristics, the findings reveal that there is no significant difference between managers employed in industry or services (as compared to the reference category, public sector) in how they evaluate the hiring desirability of early retirees. Similarly, the job level of subordinates did not significantly affect managers' decisions. In the analysis we also controlled for characteristics of managers. Neither their age nor their gender affected the hiring propensity (results not presented).

Model 3 depicts whether hiring desirability depends on organisational forces. Managers who were confronted with a structural labour force shortage during their hypothetical decision-making process were more likely to hire early retirees as compared to the reference category of organisations in need of downsizing. A similar result is observed for those organisations experiencing incidental labour force shortages. Hiring desirability drops when an organisation is in no need for new staff members, but remains positive and significant compared to the reference category.

Model 4 is the final model that includes also characteristics of applicants in the analysis. We observe that the effect of age norms remains significant even after including context information and attributes of early retirees in the analysis.

We estimated the effect of the applicants' human capital on hiring desirability. As expected, experience in a previous similar position increased early retirees' hiring chances. Potential decline of early retirees' human capital significantly lowered hiring dispositions of managers. For applicants who had not worked for one-and-a-half years, or even six months, hiring chances were substantially lower than for early retirees who had been absent for one month (reference category).

We also investigated the importance of applicants' physical appearance. In line with our expectations, managers were much more likely to hire early retirees who presented themselves as energetic. In fact, early retirees' physical appearance was the attribute that affected managers' hiring decisions the most.

Another factor evaluated in the analysis was the impact of applicants' flexibility –in terms of preferred form of appointment– on managers' hiring decisions. While applicants' willingness to work full-time did not significantly affect managers' hiring propensity, they did prefer on-call appointment above part-time and fixed-hours appointments.

Next to flexibility, we expected applicants' social capital to also be an asset in the hiring process. In line with our prediction, a recommendation by a manager's business partner increases hiring disposition. A recommendation by a manager's colleague does not have this positive effect though.

In the analysis we also evaluated the demographic characteristics of applicants. We clearly observed that the oldest category of applicants faced the greatest obstacles when returning to the labour market. A 65-year-old has lower hiring chances than a 58-year-old applicant. There was however no significant difference in how managers assessed 63-year-old applicants and their 58-years-old counterparts. Males were no more likely to be hired than females.

Our analysis also tested for the random effects of individual characteristics of early retirees, i.e. whether the effects of those characteristics differed across managers and organisations (results not shown). The analyses revealed that managers evaluated early retirees' experience and physical appearance differently. We studied additional models with cross-level interactions to account for those differences. With respect to applicants' experience, we found that managers who have higher age norms are more likely to attach higher value to applicants' experience, and that older managers attach lower value to applicants' experience while assessing the hiring desirability. With respect to the physical appearance of the applicants, we expected that the effect would differ for different sectors; our results did not support that hypothesis. We were not able to distinguish which factors influence variability in physical appearance across managers, as no interactions introduced in the analysis were significant. In the analysis we have also extensively tested for the differences in how various factors operate in different contexts but no significant results were found. Also the interaction between age norms and stereotypes that was estimated to account for independence between those constructs was not significant.

3.5.   Illustration of the effects of age norms

The last column of table 3.3 shows that the effect of age norms remains significant, even after controlling for the effect of characteristics of organisations and applicants. To illustrate the importance of manages' age norms, for each value of age norms we predicted the hiring scores (based on Model 4 in table 3.3). Based on the employability of applicants (*e.g.* capability to gain employment, maintain it or obtain new employment; Fugate *et al.*, 2004), we distinguished two categories of applicants: the 'high' and the 'low' employable. An early retiree with high employability was identified as an applicant with relevant experience, retired for a month, 58 years old and appearing energetic. An early retiree with low employability was described an applicant who did not have relevant experience, was retired for at least one-and-a-half years, was 65 years old and did not appear energetic. *Figure 3.3* presents the effect of age norms for these two categories of applicants in

Table 3.3. Results of the multilevel analysis of the hiring chance of early retirees (N=1190)

	Model 1		Model 2		Model 3		Model 4	
	Coef	t-score	Coef	t-score	Coef	t-score	Coef	t-score
Fixed effects								
Managers' characteristics								
Stereotypes								
Hard qualities			0.66	1.63	0.67	1.70	0.71	1.83
Soft qualities			-0.17	-0.65	-0.18	-0.70	-0.20	-0.80
Age norm			0.05**	2.80	0.04**	2.69	0.04*	2.41
Sector								
Industry			-0.29	-1.03	-0.29	-1.04	-0.25	-0.93
Services			-0.43	-1.70	-0.40	-1.60	-0.45	-1.81
Public			—		—		—	
Subordinates' position								
Professional			-0.60	-1.87	-0.61*	-1.96	-0.58*	-1.91
Middle			-0.46	-1.61	-0.48	-1.72	-0.55*	-2.00
Manual			—		—		—	
Organisational characteristics								
Structural shortage					1.37***	8.70	1.33***	9.48
Incidental shortage					1.23***	8.14	1.20***	8.90
No shortage					0.40*	2.59	0.38**	2.76
Need for downsizing					—		—	
Applicants' characteristics								
Age of applicant (years)								
65							-0.32**	-2.74
62							-0.12	-1.06
58							—	

	Model 1		Model 2		Model 3		Model 4	
Male[a]							0.10	1.10
Experience in similar position (yes)							0.89***	9.06
Availability								
Full-time only							-0.09	-0.62
Part-time							-0.34*	-2.41
Fixed hours							-0.50***	-3.53
Flexible appointment							—	
Last worked								
One month ago							0.53***	4.47
Six months ago							0.25*	2.06
1.5 years ago							—	
Appears energetic (yes)							1.16***	11.89
Recommended by								
A business partner							0.26*	2.28
A colleague							-0.03	-0.31
No recommendation							—	
Constant	4.15***	38.45	1.61	1.24	0.93	0.73	0.35	0.28
Random effects								
Variance level 2	2.10	0.25	1.96	0.24	1.93	0.23	1.91	0.22
Variance level 1	3.38	0.15	3.38	0.25	3.07	0.14	2.38	0.10
Model fit (degrees of freedom)	5,165.6	3	5,148.4	10	5,045.60	13	4,796.4	25

Notes: in parentheses: standard error for variance components * $p<0.05$; ** $p<0.01$; *** $p<0.001$.
[a]Ref. category: female.
Source: LISS panel study.

two organisational situations: Structural labour force shortages and need for downsizing.

The results indicate that managers' age norms are important impediments for early retirees in the labour market. For a highly employable individual applying for a position in an organisation that is in need of new staff members, we observe that the hiring desirability scores starts with a value of approximately 6.7, which is the score for the lowest age norm – *i.e.* if a manager perceives age 50 as the limit of employment. This score is just above the neutral value of 6 (on a scale running from 1 to 11). A same-category applicant dealing with managers who consider the age deadline for employment to be 80 will obtain scores approaching 8. When a highly employable applicant seeks a position in an organisation shedding jobs and when a manager holds age norms at the minimum level of 65, hiring scores peak above the neutral value of 6 and approach a value of 7. A similar effect of age norms is observed for low-employable applicants in both organisational conditions, although in those cases the hiring score does not exceed the neutral value of 6.

3.6. Discussion and conclusions

This study has investigated the effect of general attitudes of managers on their decisions to recruit early retirees. The research question was: *How do stereotypes and age norms, next to attributes of the applicants, affect managers' propensity to hire early retirees?* For this purpose a multi-method study was designed. Information on general attitudes of managers was collected in a survey (Study 1), and in a follow up vignette study (Study 2) profiles of hypothetical early retirees were presented to the same respondents, who accordingly made recruitment decisions. Data from those two sources were combined and multilevel models estimated to answer the research question.

The central issue addressed here was how general attitudes influence managers' hiring decisions. We found that managers with higher age norms (*i.e.* when a person is too old to work for 20 hours a week) were more inclined to hire early retirees. The impact of age norms clearly identifies existence of time schedules. As indicated by life-course scholars, there are informal expectations as to when behaviour should occur (Settersten, 1998), and such norms exert significant influence on life-transition behaviour (Settersten and Hagestad, 1996; Van Solinge and Henkens, 2007). Our findings thus lend support to this notion, and corroborate the link between social norms and

*Figure 3.3. Impact of the age norm on the hiring propensity of applicants
characterised by high and low employability in organisations facing
labour force shortage and need for downsizing (N=238)*

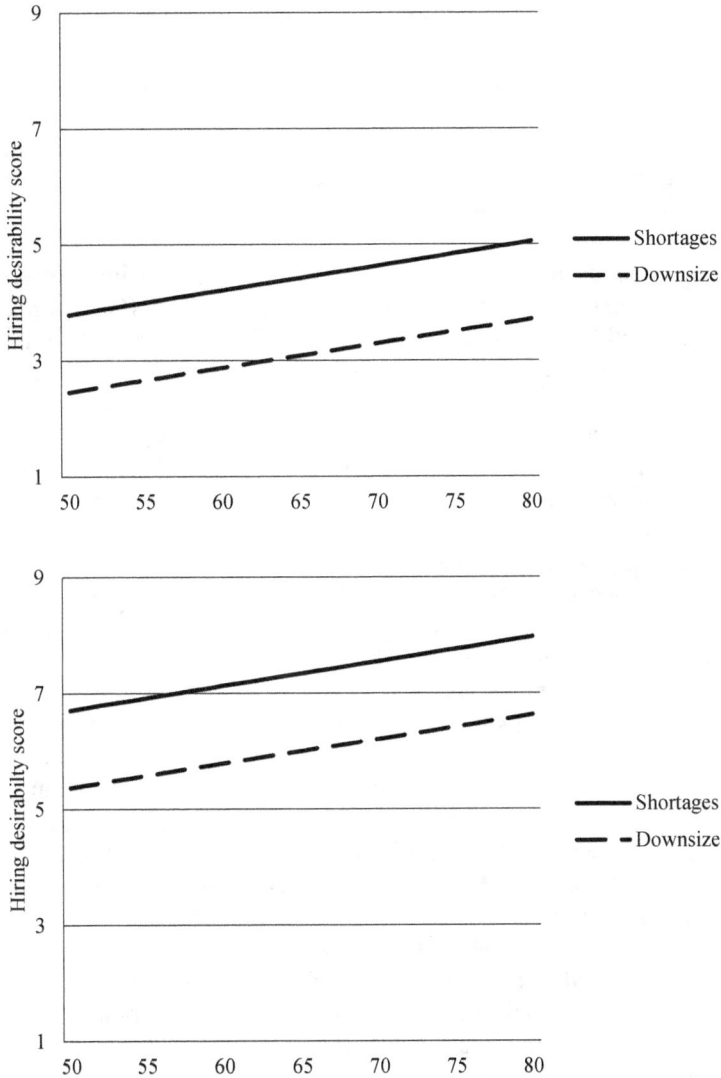

human actions that has been suggested by many theorists (Coleman, 1990; Etzioni, 2000).

The positive and significant effect of age norms on managers' hiring decisions regarding early retirees does not necessarily raise confidence in the improvement of the latter's labour market position. The overall hiring score was low. Moreover, most of the managers in our sample were convinced that the age deadline for work was 65 or younger. This suggests that although managerial norms can exert positive effects on their hiring behaviour, there is still little support for hiring workers in their late sixties.

The current study does not confirm the often-suggested link between age stereotypes and employment outcomes for older workers (Chiu *et al.*, 2001; Finkelstein and Burke, 1998; Loretto *et al.*, 2000). It has to be noted that our dependent variable refers to hiring of early retirees and not to older workers at other ages. Whether and how age stereotypes affect managers' decisions regarding different categories of older workers (unemployed, working et cetera) and different types of decisions (*e.g.* training, retaining) are important questions for future research.

Our study also shows that although stereotypes and age norms represent general attitudes towards older workers, there is only a very weak link between them. This suggests that age norms regarding retirement transitions may not be simple representations of older workers' perceived productivity. So far not much is known about the factors that affect norms of retirement transitions. To what extent age norms are culturally determined scripts and influenced by the formal age boundaries established by public and private pension schemes, or does the organisational age structure or organisational culture also affects them, are just few of possible avenues for further inquiry. Answers to those questions can offer new insights into the link between the age norms and stereotypes and consequently, their effect on employment transitions at older ages.

Despite the effect of managerial norms, importance of personal circumstances remains crucial to application success. Physical appearance and human capital are the most important factors that influenced managers' propensity to hire an early retiree. Applicants who appear vital encounter higher chances for employment. Berger (2009) showed already that many unemployed older applicants alter their physical appearance to portray a more youthful image in job interview settings to manipulate their self-presentation and sway potential employers to hire them. Our findings highlight the importance of this form of self-management on the part of older applicants, suggesting that managers indeed rely strongly on the observable attributes of early retirees when assessing their hiring desirability (Berger, 2009).

Furthermore, this study confirms the importance of human capital for the employment chances of early retirees (Karpinska *et al.*, 2011). Applicants with relevant experience were more likely to be successful in their application process. This finding implies that occupational success of early retirees is conditional on their employability (Ekerdt, 2010), highlighting the importance of skills maintenance. The emphasis on relevant experience may also limit early retirees' opportunities to work in different occupations and sectors after they retire from their career job.

Labour market participation of older workers is a growing concern of many governments. Our findings show that age norms hamper the return to the labour force. Chances of early retirees in the labour market are lower at older ages, and managers are negatively preoccupied about hiring anyone beyond a certain age. Yet, organisational forces and the individual characteristics of applicants also affect the choices managers make, showing that hiring of early retirees is a complex process. An important question is to what extent age norms will change in the near future. Will they change rapidly as a result of the changing public pension ages in Europe or will they remain unaffected? Also, will their change also apply to employees? Liefbroer (2009) showed that employees hold specific norms about appropriate timing of labour force exit. Age norms are thus woven in the broader context of work relations, indicating its complex impact on labour force outcomes.

Some practical implications of our study can be pointed out. Firstly, our findings stress the need for awareness campaigns that will demonstrate the impact of age norms in employment process. Research has shown that executives agree that older workers are discriminated against but they did not believe that this occurred in their own organisations (Maurer *et al.*, 2007). Secondly, training of recruiters towards more age awareness in selection procedures is necessary and can, in the long run, benefit both organisations and older workers by selecting better candidates and create diversity in teams. Preventing the bias that can be related to age norms has also implications for older workers who are employed in organisations. As managers have a rather clear idea as to when a person should leave the labour force, such attitudes can result in reduced access of older workers to training or lack of managerial support for employment until the statutory retirement age.

We conclude with some methodological remarks. In this article we combined survey research with vignette design. Factorial surveys are very suitable for investigating issues that are normally difficult to examine because they are rare events or involve complex multi-attribute situations (Ganong and Coleman, 2006; Wallander, 2009). Surveys, on the other hand, offer the possibility of gathering a wide range of information on context and attitudes. Although this design has clear advantages compared to single-method research design, one has to keep in mind that we asked managers to assess hypothetical situations. In addition, in our study the applicants' pool was limited to early retirees. This lowered the realism of the hiring situation. In real-life hiring participants may act or decide differently. Low hiring scores can be due to managerial comparison to other (younger) applicants, who are a natural part of the general applicants' pool.

Age discrimination is an often mentioned barrier in employment prospects of older workers (Roscigno *et al.*, 2007). Our study shows that discriminatory behaviour of managers is attributable not only to applicants' age, but is also affected by managerial norms regarding employment transitions, suggesting that age discrimination is a complex concept.

4. Retention of older workers: impact of manager's age norms and stereotypes[1]

4.1. Introduction

In many European countries pension reforms are implemented to restrict access to early exit schemes and promote longer working lives. The prolongation of working life is not only regarded as an important instrument to secure pensions in the future but also as an answer to both the expected demographically induced labour shortages as well as the changing age composition of the workforce. At the same time, survey results show that support for later retirement is relatively low among employers (Van Dalen, Henkens and Schippers, 2010a). This paper examines the factors that hamper the prolonged employment of older workers at the organisational level by looking at managers' support for older workers' retention and the factors that influence this support – or lack thereof.

The decision to retain older workers is always taken in the context of a dynamically changing organisation. A basic tenet of organisational theory is that organisations are goal-oriented systems that strive towards profit maximization, continuity, and maintenance of a healthy market position (Kalleberg, Knoke, Marsden and Spaeth, 1996). Managers are supposed to contribute to these goals by, among other things, maintaining qualified staff that contributes best to the organisational goals (Kalleberg *et al.*, 1996). Within this context, managers' dispositions towards older workers can affect workers' retention in several ways. One way is directly, as older workers are more likely to delay retirement if they think their manager supports their employment (Van Solinge and Henkens, 2007). Lack of managerial support, however, can push older workers into premature and involuntary retirement. Indirectly, managers' attitudes towards older workers' employment can determine a work environment and training possibilities for older workers that either support their prolonged employment or channel workers into retirement (Chiu, Chan, Snape and Redman, 2001).

Dispositions towards older workers and their retention are not always very positive and can lead to discriminatory attitudes and behaviours (Organisation for Economic Co-operation and Development (OECD), 2006; Van Dalen, Henkens and Schippers, 2010b). Stereotypical views of older workers are

---

[1] Will appear as: Karpinska, K., K. Henkens and J. Schippers (forthcoming), Retention of older workers: Impact of managers' age norms and stereotypes. *European Sociological Review.*

pervasive and portrait them as inflexible, less productive, more expensive than their younger colleagues, and motivated to retire as soon as possible (Chiu *et al.*, 2001; Finkelstein and Burke, 1998; Lee and Clemons, 1985; Loretto, Duncan and White, 2000; McCann and Giles, 2003; Taylor and Walker, 1998a). Age norms at the workplace also illustrate attitudes towards older workers. Age-based timetables indicate the proper age of retirement, suggesting that employment beyond that age is not desirable (Settersten and Hagestad, 1996). Although studies offer insight into general attitudes towards older workers and age norms regarding retirement, little is known about their impact on specific employment decisions regarding individual older workers and age discrimination towards older workers. Focusing on the effect of ageist stereotypes and age norms on retention allows explicit test of age discrimination in the workplace.

The evidence suggests that managers are more likely to retain older workers than to recruit them (Daniel and Heywood, 2007). Whereas the hiring decisions involve 'outsiders', *i.e.* external applicants, retention deals with 'insiders'– current staff members whose strengths and weaknesses managers were able to evaluate during the employment history. Dealing with insiders lowers the uncertainty that is a part of the hiring process. Consequently, it may restrict application of general images that are assumed to lower the transaction costs when external applicants are hired (Phelps, 1972; Van Dalen, Henkens and Schippers, 2010). Dealing with insiders also raises the issue of significance of individual characteristics. In this paper we investigate what aspects of older workers' employability –defined in terms of *e.g.* human capital, health and occupation flexibility– influence older workers' retention chances. Moreover, the question arises as to whether managers evaluate the same factors similarly for different categories of older workers. Hayward and Hardy (Hayward and Hardy, 1985) showed that determinants of early retirement vary substantially across occupational work contexts. This suggests that retention chances of low- and high-skilled workers may be determined by different factors.

To investigate what factors affect managers' retention decisions, a combination of a survey and a vignette study was designed. A factorial design (vignette study) is a method that allows the exploration of decisions in context and offers an opportunity to simulate retention decisions (Ganong and Coleman, 2006; Rossi and Anderson, 1982; Wallander, 2009). The data for our study were collected in two stages. First we carried out the survey among managers and collected information on age norms and age-related stereotypes (Study 1). A vignette study among the same group of managers

(Study 2) was conducted a month later. All managers were asked to make retention recommendations for five hypothetical workers who are eligible for early retirement. Those workers were on average 60 years old.

The study was conducted in the Netherlands. Dutch labour market policies have recently changed substantially, from support of early exit to encouragement of working longer. Over the past decades the Dutch government restricted access to disability schemes (which were often used by employers to lay off their older workers) and early retirement schemes. At the same time, financial incentives to promote prolonged employment were introduced. In 2009 about 50 percent of the workers aged 55-64 was employed (Statistics Netherlands, 2009). Although workers retire later in the Netherlands than they used to, in 2010 only 27 percent of workers retired at the statutory retirement age of 65, and the average retirement age was 63.9 (Eurostat, 2012). A recent agreement between social partners aims at a gradual increase of the eligibility for public pension benefits from the age of 65 to 67. According to the agreement, future retirement age will be interlinked with life expectancy (Government of the Netherlands, 2012).

Those policies on the macro level do not yet translate into organisational practices. Although aware of future shortages in the labour market, Dutch employers undertake limited efforts to retain their older workers (Conen, Henkens and Schippers, 2011). Only 17 percent of employers interviewed in a recent employers' study indicate they support employment of their staff until statutory retirement age. This ranks Dutch employers low among European countries. This limited support for older workers participation in the labour force and is often attributed to age discrimination. A substantial number of early retirees consider their transition into retirement as involuntary (van Solinge and Henkens, 2007) and despite policies that aim at combating age discrimination Koppes et al. (2009) showed that in the Netherlands age discrimination is still perceived to be substantial: The self-reported rate of experienced age discrimination among older (55-64 years) workers is 20 percent

4.2. Theoretical background

Managers' decisions to retain older workers eligible for early retirement can be explained from their rational considerations. In line with rational choice theory framework, in staffing decision, costs of prolonged employment are assumed to be weighed against its benefits (Coleman, 1990; Lazear,

1979). The cost-benefit balance will be affected by several groups of factors. Restrictions within organisation and restrictions in qualities of older workers influencing their (perceived) productivity will affect the retentions desirability. Manager's dispositions towards older workers are yet another aspect that is assumed to play a role here as those dispositions facilitate to the evaluation of the cost and benefits of retaining of older workers. We elaborate on all of these factors below.

4.2.1. Organisational context
The context of an organisation defines the opportunity structure for workers' retention. Macro-level developments (*e.g.* economic changes and labour force shortages) or changes in demand for output, influence managers' strategies and consequently, also employment decisions. During an economic downturn managers will need to shed jobs rather than encourage older workers to stay longer with organisations. Older workers are targeted when an organisation downsizes because due to the seniority principle their wages are often higher than those of their younger counterparts (Lazear, 1981). Also, society finds it more acceptable to make older workers redundant than younger workers (Armstrong-Stassen and Cattaneo, 2010). By contrast, managers facing structural or incidental labour force shortages may be inclined to retain their older workers to deal with workforce shortages. We therefore expect that *managers will be more inclined to recommend retention of older workers who are eligible for early retirement when the organisation faces labour force shortages.*

4.2.2. Attributes of employees
Next to the organisational forces, managers also evaluate workers' characteristics. Perceived contribution to organisational goals plays a crucial role in managers' recommendation. Workers' human capital, defined as a set of skills necessary to perform labour, is a direct measure of productivity (Becker, 1975). Although essential in the hiring process, human capital is also important when evaluating retention. In line with human capital theory (Becker, 1975), individuals' investments in human capital are made during the person's educational career. The skills and experience that are built over a long working career also have a strong influence on the individual's productivity in different roles (Eijs and Heijke, 2000; Thurow, 1975) Older workers have been accumulating their experience over the years and their specific human capital has grown considerably. Retirement of these employees would mean loss of that valuable organisation capital. We therefore expect that *managers will be more inclined to recommend retention of older workers who possess knowledge that is difficult to replace.*

Occupational flexibility is another aspect of older workers' human capital. It reflects the versatility of workers' skills and their competencies. Occupational flexibility, in the form of technical and cognitive capabilities, is crucial for organisations to cope with different corporate needs (Michellone and Zollo, 2000). The current labour markets require workers to have a broad scope of competencies while discarding the task-oriented approach towards employment. This stresses the importance of occupational flexibility for successful employment. We therefore expect that *managers will be more inclined to recommend retention of older workers who are occupationally flexible.*

Human capital may become outdated with workers' age. Updating human capital is an essential element of employee performance (Organisation for Economic Co-operation and Development (OECD), 2006). Offering training possibilities for older workers is an often-neglected avenue of human resources policies in many companies, as the expected period that the organisation can profit from the investment is relatively short in the case of workers approaching retirement (Bassanini, Booth, Brunello, De Paola and Leuven, 2005; Bishop, 1997; Organisation for Economic Co-operation and Development (OECD), 2006). And yet the evidence also suggests that older workers are not very eager to participate in skill-updating programs (Fouarge, Schils and De Grip, 2010). Workers who are not motivated to participate in training jeopardize their productivity, as they miss the opportunity to update their skills. Moreover, they are signalling low employment motivation to their employers. We therefore expect that *managers will be more inclined to recommend retention of older workers who are willing to participate in training.*

A factor not necessarily related is the health status of older workers. Poor health puts workers' productivity at risk and casts doubts on performance continuity. Although older persons are less likely to be absent due to illness, once ill they take more time to recover (Gellatly, 1995; McCann and Giles, 2002). For retention purposes, managers possess more information on the health condition of their staff than when hiring unknown applicants. Yet it is difficult to predict potential future deterioration. Managers aware of the health problems of their current staff will take this into consideration when recommending retention. We therefore predict *that managers will be more inclined to recommend retention of older workers in good health.*

Next to human capital and health issues, workers' perceived motivation to retire also plays a role in employers' retention decision. Older workers motives to retire early vary and can originate in both private and/or professional spheres. Family related factors (*i.e.* marital status, marital quality, care obligations et cetera), leisure activities, but also health problems or job demands may invoke retirement intention (see Wang and Schultz, 2010). Those personal preferences and circumstances of older workers with regard to retirement are often (implicitly) taken into consideration by their direct managers (Henkens *et al.*, 2009) and can follow different reasoning. On the one hand, managers often share an opinion that older workers have 'paid' their fair share and see workers motivation' to retire as justified. In line with this logic, early retirement is intended as a reward for workers' years of loyal service (Henkens, 2000). On the other hand, however, workers' desire to retire can be perceived by managers as a sign of low work motivation that can lead to less efficient contributions to organisational goals. Consequently, a manager will support early retirement to let go of a worker who is at risk of decreasing productivity. We therefore expect that *managers will be less likely to recommend retention of older workers who are looking out for retirement.* Retention of older workers will be also affected by their work-related behaviour and attitudes. Beehr *et al.* (1994) have described them as 'functional work relationships', *i.e.* behaviours that managers prefer or expect from their subordinates, which makes it easier to supervise them. A similar definition describes 'occupational citizenship behaviours' as behaviours that are not job-specific but which support broader organisational environment (Ng and Feldman, 2008). Examples of these behaviours and attitudes can include (but are not limited to) cooperation, conscientiousness, respect for the supervisor, not complaining about trivial matters, helping colleagues, et cetera (Beehr *et al.*, 1994; Ng and Feldman, 2008). As such, they are broader in scope than performance alone and are assumed to make managers' life easier, help achieve their goals and facilitate management. Beehr and colleagues (Beehr *et al.*, 1994) concluded that subordinates' work behaviours increased managers' satisfaction with them, which in turn may determine managers' propensity to retain older workers. We therefore expect that *managers will be more inclined to recommend retention of older workers who are easy to manage.*

4.2.3. *Dispositions of managers*
In their retention choices managers may also be affected by their dispositions towards older workers and their retention, reflected by age norms and stereotypes. Social norms are customary rules of behaviour that coordinate human interaction and can operate either as part of actors' environment or shape individuals' predispositions (Etzioni, 2000). Whatever the means of control (internal or external), sociologists, and recently also economists,

claim that social norms are an important feature that influences individuals' behaviour (Coleman, 1990; Etzioni, 2000). In the current study we focused on age norms regarding employment transitions (Settersten and Hagestad, 1996). As indicated by Van Solinge and Henkens (2007), norms illustrate the appropriate time to retire. Older workers compare themselves to existing social timetables to decide if they should exit the labour force, and act accordingly. Managers' age norms towards older workers' retirement are assumed to affect retention of older workers similarly. Managers will encourage employment when they believe it is still appropriate. While age norms about the 'right time' to retire are formally expressed in age boundaries established by public and private pension schemes, the customary age norms held by managers do not necessarily follow that lead. We therefore hypothesize that *managers who have a higher age norm with respect to retirement timing will be more inclined to recommend retention of older workers.*

Stereotypes are another aspect of managers' dispositions. Well-documented evidence suggests that employers often see older workers as inflexible, unwilling (or unable) to adapt to the changing work environment, and less productive than their younger colleagues. The same studies confirm, however, that older workers are valued for their trustworthiness, specific knowledge and interpersonal skills (Chiu *et al.*, 2001; Finkelstein and Burke, 1998; Lee and Clemons, 1985; Loretto, Duncan and White, 2000; McCann and Giles, 2002; Taylor and Walker, 1998a). Van Dalen *et al.* (2010b) have captured this dual aspect of stereotypes regarding older workers' productivity. They showed that employers' attitudes towards older workers reflect two dimensions: Hard and soft skills. Soft skills are defined as qualities that can be characterized as 'organisational citizenship behaviour' – pro-social behaviour that is not job-specific but which supports the broader organisational environment in which jobs are performed (Ng and Feldman, 2008; Van Dalen *et al.*, 2010b). Hard skills, on the contrary, reflect mental and physical capacity, willingness to learn new skills and to adapt to new technologies, and flexibility. One important aspect of stereotypes is that prevailing views may affect managers' discriminatory attitudes and behaviour (Chiu *et al.*, 2001). We therefore expect that *managers who have more positive perceptions of older workers' hard and soft skills will be more inclined to recommend retention of older workers.*

4.2.4.   Difference between low- and high-skilled workers
Demands from older workers depend greatly on their ability to meet job requirements, both mentally and physically. As different occupations require different skills in their daily routine, retention chances of different categories

of older workers will also differ. Employer surveys indicate that managers are less likely to embrace older low-skilled workers than older professionals (Munnell, Sass and Soto, 2006). Low-skilled workers work disproportionately more in physically demanding jobs than those with more education (Eyster, Johnson and Toder, 2008). Consequently, a good health situation is assumed to be more important for low-skilled older workers' productivity than for that of high-skilled workers. For high-skilled older workers, job-specific knowledge is assumed to be more important that for low-skilled workers. We therefore predict that *retention chances of low-skilled older workers will be more affected by their health than the chances of high-skilled workers.*

4.3.   Data and methods

To answer the research questions, a combination of survey research (Study 1) with a factorial study (Study 2) was designed. First a survey was administered to managers, and one month later the same managers were approached again to complete a vignette study. With this one-month gap between the studies we limited the risk of bias related to potential carryover effects that can occur if the same respondents are subject to two experimental conditions (Leeuw, Hox and Dillman, 2008). We collected the data by accessing the sample of the Longitudinal Internet Studies for the Social Sciences of Tilburg University (http://www.lissdata.nl/lissdata/). LISS is an Internet panel that consists of 5.000 households, comprising 8.000 individuals. All individuals were selected based on a true probability sample of households drawn from the population register by Statistics Netherlands.

4.3.1.   Study 1
During Study 1, panel members who held a managerial position at the time of the study were identified and presented with questions on stereotypes regarding older workers, age norms and background characteristics. The data was collected in April 2010.

Participants
Based on the question: *Do you supervise others?*, a total of 700 LISS members were approached (the exact number of managers in the LISS is not known). The response rate for Study 1 was 73.6 percent (N=515). Although the study was aimed at different-level managers in organisations, not all of the respondents satisfied this condition. Further selection based on the questions: *What is your current occupation?* and *Do you supervise others?* eliminated 191 non-managers from the sample. In total, 324 managers participated in

Study 1. Those managers were approached a month later to participate in Study 2. The final sample consisted of 238 managers and included managers who participated in both studies. The attrition between Study 1 and 2 was not related to respondents' age, gender, education level or position occupied. Three categories of managers are represented according to the LISS panel distinction:[2] *Higher supervisory positions* (manager, director, owner of large company, supervisory civil servant; N=99), *intermediate supervisory or commercial positions* (head representative, department manager, shopkeeper; N=99) and *supervisory manual workers* (N=40). The sample consisted of 182 males and 56 females, and the mean age of respondents was 45.3 (range 24-65, SD=9.45). For details see *table 4.1*.

Measurements
Existing age norms are measured on the basis of the open question: *At what age do you consider a person too old to work in your organisation for 20 hours a week or more?* The answer ranged from 40 to 100. To avoid problems with outliers, answers were truncated between 50 and 80. The sensitivity analyses proved this coding to be robust. The mean of the age managers responded in the total sample was 64.7 years with a SD of 5.9. Modal value of age was 65 –approximately 32 percent of respondents indicated that the retirement age of 65 is when a person is too old to work 20 hours or more. We have also computed means for the separate subsamples– managers who supervise low- and high-skilled workers. The age norm for managers predominantly supervising low-skilled workers was 63.9 (SD =6.62), while for those who supervised high-skilled workers it was 64.6 (SD= 5.89). *Figure 4.1* presents the distribution of the answers for the total sample of managers.

Stereotypes were measured with two questions. First we asked: *To what extent do the following characteristics apply to workers aged 60 or older?* And: *To what extent do the following characteristics apply to workers aged 35 and younger?* The characteristics presented in both questions were: *Flexibility, social skills, commitment to organisation, creativity, management skills, reliability, willingness to learn, physical capacity, resistance to stress, new technological skills.* The answer categories were (1) hardly, (2) somewhat, (3) strongly, and (4) very strongly. For the distribution of answers see *figure 4.2*.

Based on the factor analysis, two factors were selected: *Soft and hard skills* (Van Dalen *et al.*, 2010b). In the consecutive analyses relative scores scales –

---

[2]   For distinctions between respondents' professions see: http://www.lissdata.nl/dataarchive/study_
    units/view/145

Table 4.1. Descriptive statistics, N=238

	Min	Max	Mean/%	St. Dev.
Dependent variable				
Retention recommendation[a]				
Total sample	1	11	5.09	2.52
Low-skilled workers	1	11	5.22	2.39
High-skilled workers	1	11	5.06	2.55
Independent variables				
Dispositions				
Stereotypes- relative scores				
Hard qualities[b] - total sample	0.33	3.5	0.68	0.27
Hard qualities - low-skilled workers			0.74	0.24
Hard qualities - high shilled workers			0.66	0.27
Soft qualities[c] - total sample	0.28	2.33	1.16	0.41
Soft qualities - low skilled workers			1.15	0.44
Soft qualities - high skilled workers			1.16	0.40
Age norm				
Total sample	50	80	64.5	6.04
Low-skilled workers	50	80	63.9	6.62
High-skilled workers	50	80	64.6	5.89
Characteristics of respondents				
Managerial position				
Higher supervisory positions	0	1	41.5	
Intermediate supervisory or	0	1	41.5	
commercial positions				
Supervisory manual workers	0	1	16.8	
Age (years)	24	65	45.3	9.4
Male	0	1	76.4	
Education (years)	8	18	15.5	2.55
Job level of subordinates				
Low-skilled	0	1	18.9	
High-skilled	0	1	81.1	
Size of organisation	10	10,000	375.8	1,048.54
Sector				
Industry	0	1	26.4	
Services	0	1	38.8	
Public	0	1	34.8	

[a] (1)Retaining very undesirable-(11) Retaining very undesirable; [b](0.33) Hard skills applying more to older workers-(3.5) Hard skills applying more to younger workers; [c] (0.33) Soft skills applying more to older workers-(2.3) Soft skills applying more to younger workers.
Source: LISS panel study.

Figure 4.1. Distribution of age norms held by managers in the LISS sample

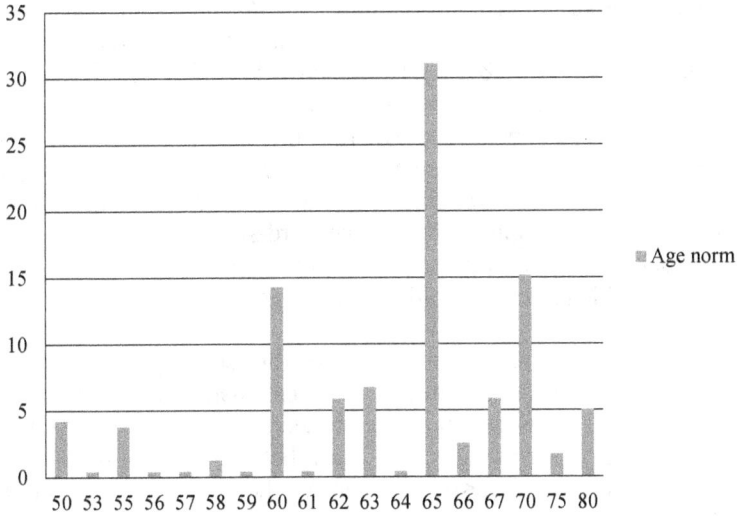

Source: LISS panel study.

Figure 4.2. Stereotypes held by managers about older- and younger workers

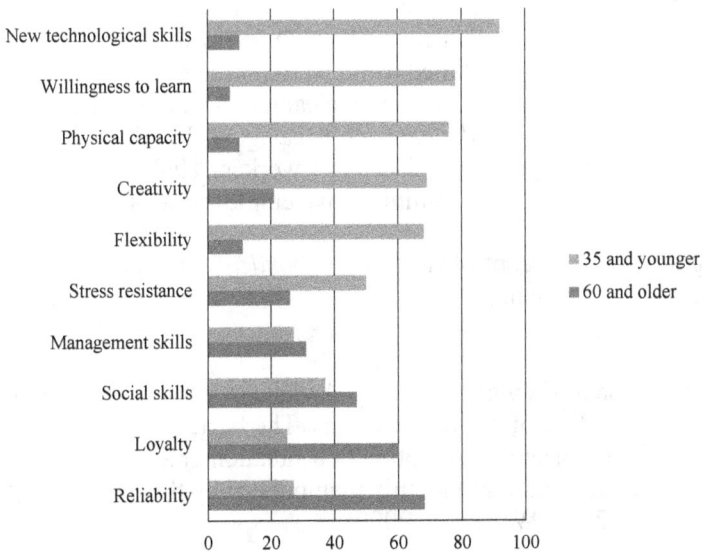

Source: LISS panel study.

level to which those characteristics apply to older workers compared to their younger counterparts– were computed. The *soft skills* scale consists of the following four items: *social skills, commitment to organisation, management skills, reliability* (range 0.28-2.33; Cronbach's alpha=0.859). The mean value exceeds 1 (M=1.16, SD=0.41), implying that on average workers aged 60 or older were perceived to possess those skills more than younger workers. The *hard skills* scale is based on these items: *Creativity, flexibility, willingness to learn, physical capacity, resistance to stress, new technological skills* (range 0.33-3.5, Cronbach's alpha=0.839). The hard-skills scale is lower than 1 (M=0.68, SD=0.27), meaning that on average managers consider those skills as more applicable to younger rather than older workers.

To rule out multicolinearity problems between age stereotypes and age norms, correlations between those concepts were calculated. The results indicate that stereotypes as measured in this study were not strongly correlated with the measure of age norms. The correlation between the soft-qualities scale and age norm was 0.157 (p<0.001), and for the hard-qualities scale it was 0.126 (p<0.001).

Subordinates' position level was determined by the question: *What is the required education level for the position you supervise most often?* Following earlier studies (Steedman and McIntosh, 2001), we defined *low-skilled workers* as those in occupations requiring primary or lower secondary education (equivalent of ISCED levels 0, 1 and 2). In total 45 managers supervised low-skilled workers. Represented occupations included packaging positions, gardening, street cleaning. All other educational levels were included in the *high-skilled workers* category (ISCED 3 and higher). In the sample 193 managers supervised those workers. High-skilled occupations were diverse, ranging from administrative employees to scientists.

During this study the control variables *respondents' gender and respondents' age* were also collected.

4.3.2.   Study 2
Study 2 consisted of a vignette survey. A vignette study is a method intended for the investigation of human decisions. The basic item of the survey is a vignette, which is a short description of a situation or a person, generated by combining characteristics randomly manipulated by the researcher (Ganong and Coleman, 2006; Wallander, 2009).

Participants
For Study 2, all respondents who participated in the first round were contacted to participate in the vignette survey. A total of 238 managers participated and the response rate for Study 2 was 82.3 percent. In Study 2 each manager judged 5 vignettes, resulting in a total of 1190 vignettes.

Measurements
In Study 2 various hypothetical older workers who were eligible for early retirement were described by several characteristics. The retention situation was placed in a specific context. The eight vignette characteristics were: *organisational context* (organisation facing structural labour force shortages, incidental labour force shortages, no labour force shortages, need for downsizing); *knowledge and experience* (difficult to replace/not difficult to replace); *occupational flexibility* (yes/no); *attitude towards retirement* (looking forward to it/ not looking forward); *health condition* (healthy/frail); *motivation to participate in training* (high, average, low); *manageability* (employee easy to manage, sometimes not easy to manage, difficult to manage). In the vignettes we also included *worker's age* (59, 61, 63 and 65). Given all possible combinations of the variables and their respective levels, the universe of 2.304 unique vignettes was created (*i.e.* 4x2x4x2x2x2x3x3; for details see *table 4.2*). None of the vignettes contained impossible combination of the factors.

In a vignette survey only a random selection from the vignette universe is judged by respondents (Wallander, 2009). In our study, each participant received a random sample of 5 vignettes (random selection with replacement). The instruction was as follows:

Below you can find the description of older workers who are eligible for early retirement. Please indicate, for each profile, what is the likelihood of you willing to retain that older worker for a few more years in your organisation for the position you supervise most often.

Each manager rated each vignette on an 11-point scale, ranging from 1 (retaining very undesirable) to 11 (retaining very desirable). *Figure 4.3* presents an example of a vignette used in the study.

4.3.3.   Analyses
In a vignette design, the unit of analysis is the vignette (Coleman, 1990; Ganong and Coleman, 2006). As each manager judged five vignettes, our survey data have a hierarchical structure by design, therefore observations are

Table 4.2. Organisational contexts and job applicants' attributes in the vignette

Item	Categories
Organisation	
Organisational context	Structural labour force shortages
	Incidental labour force shortages
	No labour force shortages
	Need for downsizing
Employee	
Knowledge and experience	Difficult to replace
	Not diffucult to replace
Age (years)	59
	61
	63
	65
Occupationally flexible	Yes
	No
Attitude towards retirement	Looking forward
	Not looking forward
Health	Healthy
	Frail
Willingness to participate in training	High
	Average
	Low
Manageability	Employee easy to manage
	Employee occasionally difficult to manage
	Employee difficult to manage

Source: LISS panel study.

not independent (Wallander, 2009). Multilevel models were applied to deal with the hierarchical structure of the data (Hox, 2002). Fixed models were estimated. Level-2 variables included in each model comprised variables at the level of managers (managers' dispositions and their demographic characteristics), level-1 variables consisted of individual attributes of older workers that were included in vignettes. All the variables measured in Study 2 were included in the analysis as dummy variables, so the weights estimated for each dummy variable are comparable. For the sake of simplicity, the stepwise model estimation is not presented (details of the analysis available upon request). This study also looked at differences in evaluations of low-

Figure 4.3. Example of a vignette

Below you can find the description of older workers who are eligible for early retirement. Please indicate, for each profile, what is the likelihood of you willing to retain that older worker for a few more years in your organisation for the position you supervise most often?

Context:

| Organisational context | Structural labour-force shortage |

Applicant:

Knowledge difficult to replace | Yes

Age (Years) | 65

Occupationally flexible | Yes

Attitude towards retirement | Looking forward

Health | Good

Willingness to participate in training | Low

Managing employee | Employee occasionally difficult to manage

What is the likelihood of you would willing to retain that older worker for few more years in your organisation for the position you most often supervise?

1	2	3	4	5	6	7	8	9	10	11
Retaining very undesirable					Neutral				Retaining very desirable	

and high-skilled workers, and separate models were estimated for both groups. Testing for equality of the coefficients between both subsamples was done with the Chow test (Gould, 2002; Steedma and McIntosh, 2001).

4.4. Results

First, we estimated an empty model for the total sample that decomposed the variance between the two levels of analysis (results not presented). The intercepts showed that, on a scale ranging from 1 to 11, retention desirability for older workers was 5.09. An interclass correlation indicated that approximately 25 percent of the total variance was accounted for by the grouping of the data. The hiring recommendation did differ between managers, although most variation existed among managers, *i.e.* at the level of vignette.

Table 4.3 reports the results of the analysis. The first column presents the results for the total sample, while columns 2 and 3 show the estimated results of separate analyses for the subsamples of low- and high- skilled workers, respectively.

The analysis looked at three groups of factors to explain managers' retention recommendation: organisational context, characteristics of older workers and managers's individual characteristics and dispositions. With respect to organisational context, we found that managers were more likely to recommend retention if their organisation faced labour force shortages. That applies to structural as well as incidental labour force shortages. Organisations facing no such shortage did not differ significantly from the reference category of organisations in need of downsizing.

With respect to older workers' characteristics, our analysis confirmed the importance of human capital for retention. Older workers were more likely to get retained if they were healthy and when their knowledge was difficult to replace. Moreover, workers' attitudes also contributed to their retention chances. Workers who were highly or moderately willing to participate in training were more likely to get retention recommendation than their unmotivated counterparts. Looking forward to retirement decreased workers' chances for retention. Older workers who were easy to manage or caused managing difficulties only occasionally were more likely to be retained than more difficult colleagues. In the analysis we also controlled for workers' age. Workers faced lower chances for retention if they were 65 years old as compared to workers at age 59. For all other age categories no significant differences with the reference category were found.

Next to organisational and individual attributes we also estimated the impact of managerial dispositions on retention of older workers. Age norms did affect managers' retention recommendations: managers who held higher age norms about the appropriate time to retire were more likely to recommend retention. Next to norms, the effect of age stereotypes was also estimated. Contrary to our expectations, perception of hard skills was not a significant predictor of managerial recommendations. Conversely, managers who perceived older workers to possess more soft qualities than younger workers were more likely to recommend their retention.

To sum up, our study shows that various factors affect older workers' chances for retentions. Our analysis confirmed the hypothesis on the importance of organisational circumstances on retention of older workers. With respect to characteristics of older workers themselves, most of our hypotheses were supported; the study shows that human capital of older workers, their health status, flexibility, attitudes towards retirement, training motivation and manageability contribute to their retention chances. Human capital that was difficult to replace was especially important as a condition for older workers' retention. We also estimated the effect of managers' discriminatory attitudes towards older workers on their decisions. The analysis showed that in their decision managers are guided by normative perceptions of older workers employment. Moreover, the perception of the productivity of older workers, as expressed by soft qualities, was shown to affect managers' decisions.

In the analysis we also controlled for individual characteristics of managers. Neither their age nor their gender affected retention propensity. With respect to organisation characteristics, the findings reveal that there was no significant difference between managers employed in industry or services (as compared to the reference category, public sector) in how they evaluate retention desirability of older workers (results not shown).

Our analysis also tests for the random effects of individual characteristics of older workers, *i.e.* whether the effects of those characteristics differ across managers and organisations (results not shown). None of the random effects was significant, indicating that managers evaluate individual factors similarly.

Differences between low- and high-skilled workers
To establish whether the factors influencing attitudes towards retention of older workers differ between managers supervising low- and high-skilled workers, separate analyses were estimated for both subsamples. The results are presented in columns 2 and 3 of table 4.3. The results of the Chow test indicate that neither of the evaluated factors differed significantly in evolutions managers made of low- and high-skilled workers: Managers thus assigned fairly consistent weights to factors included in the analysis.

The sensitivity tests were conducted in the consecutive steps. In our model we included several interaction terms of our predictor variables with a continuous measure of job level (ISCED). These interaction terms proved to be non-significant. As such, the results of those analyses (available upon

Table 4.3. results of the multilevel analysis of the retention recommendation

	Total workers		Low-skilled		Highly-skilled	
	Coef	t-score	Coef	t-score	Coef	t-score
Fixed effects						
Organisational context						
Structural labour force shortage[a]	1.15**	7.32	1.39***	4.04	1.08***	6.12
Incidental labour force shortage	0.97**	6.22	0.84*	2.40	1.00***	5.79
No labour force shortage	0.25	1.61	-0.12	-0.34	0.33	1.91
Need for downsizing	—		—		—	
Employees' attributes						
Knowledge and experience						
Difficult to replace	1.52***	13.51	1.14***	4.61	1.61***	12.70
Not difficult to replace	—		—		—	
Employee's age (years)						
65	-0.83***	-5.31	-0.39	-1.16	-0.92***	-5.22
63	-0.18	-1.17	0.03	0.08	-0.21	-1.23
61	-0.11	-0.75	-0.18	-0.56	-0.08	-0.51
59						
Occupationally flexible (ref. no.)	0.464***	4.16	0.63*	2.56	0.42***	3.41
Attitude towards retirement						
Looking forward	-0.72***	-6.52	-1.00***	-4.14	-0.66***	-5.41
Not looking forward						
Good health (ref. frail)	0.91***	8.19	0.82***	3.38	0.91***	7.23
Willingness to participate in training						
High	0.68***	5.02	0.99***	3.36	0.61***	4.01
Moderate	0.44***	3.29	0.680*	2.29	0.40**	2.67
Low	—		—		—	

Managing an employee						
Easy to manage	0.77***	5.66	0.64*	2.05	0.80***	5.23
Occasionally difficult to manage	0.62***	4.54	0.98***	3.38	0.51***	3.33
Difficult to manage	—		—		—	
Managers' characteristics						
Age norm	0.06***	3.94	0.05	1.70	0.06***	3.61
Hard stereotypes	-0.46	-1.27	-1.18	-1.19	-0.34	-0.87
Soft stereotypes	0.56*	2.35	0.39	0.76	0.67*	2.51
Age	0.00	0.57	0.03	1.63	0.00	0.02
Male (ref. female)	0.31	1.37	0.61	1.16	0.25	0.99
Low-skilled workers (ref. high-skilled workers)	0.30	1.24				
Constant	-2.28	-1.87	-2.49	-1.00	-2.32	-1.77
Random effects						
Variance level 2	1.54	0.201	1.37	0.41	1.54	0.22
Variance level 1	3.12	0.143	2.66	0.28	3.18	0.16
Model fit (degrees of freedom)	-2515.88	20	-458.03	19	-2046.62	19
N of vignettes (N of respondents)	1190	238	255	45	965	193

Notes: In parentheses: standard error for variance components, * $p<0.05$; ** $p<0.01$; *** $p<0.001$.

request) did not differ from earlier tests and indicate that our explanatory model did not differ significantly between higher- and lower-skilled workers in our data.

4.4.1.   Retention of older workers

The analysis has shown that various factors contribute to managers' retention recommendations. To illustrate the importance of the different groups of explanatory variables, retention recommendation scores were predicted for various market conditions and managers' norms about retirement age, based on the full model presented in table 4.3. Older workers were defined in terms of their employability, *e.g.* the ability to secure and maintain employment (Fugate, Kinicki and Ashforth, 2004). We defined workers with *high employability* as those whose experience was difficult to replace and were versatile in their tasks, healthy, willing to participate in training and motivated to stay employed. Workers characterized by *low employability* did not have experience that was difficult to replace, were not occupationally flexible, were in frail health, were not willing to participate in training and were looking forward to retirement. *Table 4.4* depicts the predicted scores.

The results show that in the situation where organisations shed jobs and managers' age norm was low (*i.e.* 50 years), the predicted retention recommendation score for highly employable older workers was just above the neutral value – 6.3, on a scale to 11. This score rose substantially to 8.2 when managers' age norm increased to 80. Chances of highly employable workers for retention increased even further –to 9.3– when organisations faced labour force shortages. Low-employable older workers in organisations that needed to shed jobs, supervised by a manager who held age norms of 50, received a score of 3.5. Their low retention chances did not exceed the neutral value even when managers's age norms increased to 80 and the organisation faced structural labour force shortages. In short, these results suggest that

Table 4.4. Predicted scores of retention recommendation for high- and low-employable workers in different organisational settings

	High-employable worker	Low-employable worker
Downsizing - age norm low (age 50)	6.3	2.4
Downsizing - age norm high (age 80)	8.2	4.3
Labour force shortage - age norm high (age 80)	9.3	5.4

the employment opportunities for high-employable older workers are to a large extent dependent on labour market circumstances and existing age norms within organisations. Older workers with low employability have few opportunities even when there are labour market shortages and few normative barriers to their employment.

4.5.   Discussion and conclusions

The current study focused on the factors that affect managers' recommendations to retain older workers eligible for early retirement. To examine this issue, a combination of a survey and vignette research was designed. The data was collected among a sample of 238 managers in various Dutch organisations and multilevel models were estimated. The study shows that managers' attitudes towards retention of older workers are influenced by labour market conditions (in particular labour force shortages), individual attributes of older workers, and dispositions of managers.

With respect to managers' dispositions, our study showed that age norms regarding retirement significantly affected managers' recommendations to retain older workers. Managers who held higher age norms were much more likely to support an employee's retention. Despite this positive result, managerial support for prolonged employment of older workers seems rather limited, with few managers supporting work beyond the age of 65. Managers' normative dispositions do not yet follow the institutional changes that rise public pension eligibility age to 67 (Stichting van de Arbeid, 2011). These dispositions can thus form an obstacle for the employment of older workers; our study shows that discriminatory behaviour of managers is also affected by managerial norms regarding employment transitions.

We assume in this paper and found empirical support for the notion that age norms influence employment decisions towards older workers. In our analysis we measured the existing norms one month before we presented our respondents with the profiles of hypothetical older workers. In our study we treat age norms as given. However, the relation between age norms and employment decisions might also take a reversed form, i.e. managers who are willing to retain particular older workers might shift their norms accordingly. In fact age norms will not be carved in stone. Norms might change over time due to changing circumstances and institutional arrangements and age and educational structure of the workforce. Among these circumstances might also be the supervision of respected older workers one wants to retain. The extent to which this mechanism is important in the explanation of age norms and their changes over time is an interesting area for further inquiry.

Next to the effect of age norms, managers' general perceptions of older workers were evaluated. These general attitudes regarding the productivity of older workers did not have a major influence on managers' ratings of individual vignettes. Perception of hard qualities did not significantly affect retention recommendations of managers, while a slight positive effect was found for the perception of soft qualities. In an earlier study Henkens (2005) showed that perception of stereotypes did affect managers' general opinions about the retention desirability of older workers. Similarly, Chiu et al. (2001) concluded that stereotypes are related to discriminatory work attitudes managers hold towards older workers. The current analysis suggests that general stereotype attitudes of managers do not influence their specific retention recommendation when more information on workers' individual attributes and the opportunity structure in the organisation is available.

The study shed more light on older workers' chances of postponing their retirement, and shows that older workers who intend to remain active in the labour market until their statutory retirement age are confronted with various restrictions. Retention of older workers was largely affected by their own circumstances. Our study demonstrates that low-employable workers have very limited chances of remaining employed, even if the labour market conditions and the dispositions of managers are positive. Even if workers do posses valuable assets, their chances for retention remain highly dependent on the organisational context and the dispositions of managers. The results suggest that although skills maintenance and lifelong learning are a key to older workers' labour force participation, the restrictions present in the labour market are crucial when retention is considered. Van Solinge and Henkens (2007) already concluded that substantial numbers of older workers have limited agency over their retirement transitions. Our study confirms that view, showing that organisational context and negative attitudes of managers form a barrier to workers' prolonged employment.

Furthermore, our study revealed that managers evaluated various attributes similarly, regardless of the position level of their subordinates. This suggests that low- and high-skilled workers face the same type of restrictions in the labour force. Our study did not aim at estimating differences in retention of low- and high-skilled workers. Establishing what the retention chances are for those groups is an interesting avenue for future research.

We conclude with some methodological remarks. We combined survey research with a vignette design, which we see as a noteworthy strength of this study. Vignette surveys are suitable for investigating decisions that are normally difficult to examine because they are rare events or involve complex multi-attribute situations (Ganong and Coleman, 2006; Wallander, 2009). Surveys, on the other hand, offer the possibility of gathering a wide range of information on context and general attitudes.

Although our design has clear advantages compared to a single-method research design, there are some limitations of this approach. While this design offers the possibility to model the impact of general attitudes on retention of specific older workers, we cannot rule out the risk of social desirability bias that might have occurred when managers were primed with the survey and later asked to participate in the vignette experiment (Pager and Quillian, 2005). Moreover, there is evidence that vignette studies may lead to underestimation of the discriminatory attitudes in employment decisions as compared to field studies (Pager and Quillian, 2005). Also, one has to keep in mind that we asked managers to assess hypothetical situations. In real life hiring participants may act or decide differently.

Gender was not included in the study design. Labour market participation of older woman is still relatively low in the Netherlands (in 2009 approximately 18 percent of women aged 60-65 were active in the labour force, Statistics Netherlands 2010). Including gender in the vignettes would have resulted in unrealistic experiment settings and might have contaminated the results. As a result, we are not able to investigate whether managers differ in their judgment of male versus female older workers, which can be a considered a limitation of this study.

Last but not least, our study was conducted in 2010, in the midst of the global financial crisis. During the data collection unemployment rates in the Netherlands were still low but there was already growing pessimism among employers about future economic opportunities and many firms already limited the hiring of new staff. We cannot exclude the possibility that our results partly reflect these worries and underestimated the structural chances of retention of older workers.

Changes in labour market regulations, with an increased retirement age and the abolishment of mandatory retirement, lead to a deinstitutionalisation of retirement, with more variation in retirement choices for older workers. Retirement becomes an outcome of workers' plans and employment opportunities provided by employers. In this changing context, insight into managers' attitudes is increasingly important. Karpinska *et al.* (Karpinska, Henkens and Schippers, forthcoming) showed how re-employment opportunities for early retirees were restricted by managerial dispositions towards older workers. This paper shows that these dispositions also influence the employment prospects of insiders who are still employed. Combating age discrimination in the labour market and changing the dispositions of managers towards older workers is therefore highly relevant for increasing their labour market participation.

In the current study we have examined factors that affect retention of older workers in the context of the Dutch labour market. Yet, all European countries are confronted with ageing of the labour force and will have to face the challenge of prolonging of older people' working lives in order to secure financial stability and solidity of the welfare state. Although presented results offer a valuable insight into labour market participation at older ages, it should be noted that those results cannot be generalizable to countries with different legal arrangements. In the Netherlands as well as the other European countries the pension system is linked to mandatory retirement, while in the United States mandatory retirement because of age is not allowed. This arrangement can affect retention of managers; supervisors know that, even if they discourage early retirement of their subordinates, all older workers will have to retire at age of 65. Future research must show the extent to which the conclusions drawn in this study also hold in situations where no mandatory retirement age exists.

5. Training opportunities for older workers in the Netherlands. A policy capturing study[1]

5.1. Introduction

Training is clearly essential for workers and organisations: It helps workers maintain and increase their employability, enhances their motivation and job satisfaction, and at the same time also benefits the organisations that employ them (Becker, 1975). Aguinis and Kraiger pointed out that "as organisations strive to compete in the global economy, differentiation on the basis of the skill, knowledge, and motivation of their workforce takes on increasing importance," stressing the significance of updating workers' skills (Aguinis and Kraiger, 2009, p. 452).

Different surveys of working populations in the European Union focus on worker training activities and show that approximately 39 percent of European adults participated in training (Dohmen and Timmermann, 2010). The evidence suggests that participation in training is rather voluntary, as only approximately 20 percent of respondents who followed training did so because it was obligatory (Dohmen and Timmermann, 2010) or enforced by collective agreements, et cetera (Leuven and Oosterbeek, 1999). Although the numbers vary per country, it is clear that not all workers are offered the possibility to participate in training. Leuven and Oosterbeek (1999) pointed out that employers initiate training more often than employees, stressing managers' role in offering training opportunities. However, it is still unclear how managers arrive at their decision regarding to whom such opportunities should be offered to.

Different domains of social sciences have accumulated evidence regarding various aspects of training. Psychological studies focus extensively on training design and transfer, its delivery and evaluation, and improvement of performance (*e.g.*, Brown and Sitzmann, 2011). Aguinis and Kraiger (2009) discuss comprehensively the benefits of training for individuals, teams and organisations, stressing the importance of knowledge transition and increased performance. The question of training participation is mostly framed in terms of needs assessment and workers' readiness to participate in training (defined as motivation and self-beliefs that are likely to influence

---

[1] A revised version of this chapter is submitted to Journal of Occupational Behavior as: Karpinska, K., K. Henkens, J. Schippers and M. Wang. Training opportunities for older workers in the Netherlands. A policy capturing study.

willingness to attend training and learning during training) (Aguinis and Kraiger, 2009). Economists focus mostly on returns to training and reports consistently positive relationships between training participation and wages (Leuven and Oosterbeek, 2004). Finally, sociologists examine the patterns of participation, education and status attainment related to training and internal labor market access to it (*e.g.*, Rainbird, 2000). However, few previous studies from theses research domains have focused on the distribution of training opportunities (*i.e.*, who receives training). Recently Lazazzara, Karpinska, Henkens (2012) have argued that not all workers are offered equal opportunities when it comes to access to training. Following this observation, the current study aims to examine factors that may affect manager's decisions to grant training opportunities to older workers.

Participation in training is especially important for older workers. An ageing workforce requires older workers to prolong their working careers to assure sufficient labor market supply and the sustainability of social security systems. One of the conditions of productive retention is training: It offers older workers opportunities to maintain and enhance their employment potential and optimize their value in the labor market (Cully, VandenHeuvel, Wooden and Curtain, 2001; OECD, 2006). Yet, a wide body of evidence suggests that training incidences decrease with age (Armstrong-Stassen and Templer, 2005; Bishop, 1997) and that employers' discriminatory attitudes and their perception of the productive potential of older workers form barriers to training (Cully *et al.*, 2001). Many studies indicate that employers see older workers as inflexible, unwilling (or unable) to adapt to the changing work environment and less productive than their younger colleagues (Chiu *et al.*, 2001). Such discriminatory attitudes of managers can affect their decisions with respect to older workers (Chiu *et al.*, 2001). The evidence suggests that managers are often not very positive in their evaluation of training for older workers (Loretto and White, 2006), and conveys an idea that older workers are excluded from training based on their age (Eurobarometer, 2012). The research question we pose in this study is: *What are the factors that affect training opportunities for older workers?*

Something that complicates a comprehensive view of the factors that might influence training opportunities is the huge variety of types of training and the investments involved. Most studies report information on formal and specific training, i.e. training that can be applied only at the company that provides it (Becker, 1975; Leuven and Oosterbeek, 1999). Less is known about different types of training and whether those differences affect managers' propensity to offer such opportunities to older workers. This study aims at examining training of older workers with a broader empirical basis by testing hypotheses on different types of training settings.

Our study contributes to the literature in three ways. Firstly, the study integrates two theoretical perspectives to the impact of workers' characteristics on training opportunities. Human capital theory frames training as an investment in employees that benefits both the employee and the organisation (Becker, 1975). Social exchange theory, however, frames training as a reward for worker performance (Cropanzano and Mitchell, 2005). This approach challenges the dominant neo-classical economic approach to training and offers a chance to test its predictions. Secondly, next to the effects of workers' characteristics, also restrictions present in the organisations and managers' characteristics are included in the analysis of the training opportunities. This focus offers comprehensive view on factors that affect training opportunities. Thirdly, we examine managers' propensity to offer older workers training in different situations; investigated conditions include specific training aimed at increasing skills in employees' current position, but also factors that affect more general training aimed at internal mobility, and in different financial settings. This allows us to examine training opportunities depending on their context.

To investigate factors that affect training opportunities for older workers we conducted a survey among 153 managers in different sectors of the Dutch economy. The respondents were employed in various organisations, and occupied managerial positions at different levels in the organisational structure. All respondents were responsible for supervising others. The survey was combined with a vignette experiment during which managers were presented with profiles of older workers and were asked how likely it was they would offer training to those workers.

The study was carried out in the Netherlands, where labor market policies have recently changed substantially from encouragement of early exit to encouragement to work longer. A recent policy change enforces extending working lives until the age of 67. The Netherlands is however still characterized by low job mobility among older workers (OECD, 2006), and age discrimination is one of the forces assumed to be behind this phenomenon. Despite policies aimed at combating age discrimination, Koppes et al. (2008) showed that in the Netherlands age discrimination is still perceived to be substantial, at a self-reported rate among older workers (ages 55-64) of 20 percent.

On-the-job training in the Netherlands is predominantly offered and paid for by organisations, and employees follow it during their working hours. In general, participation rates in training are relatively high; approximately 53 percent of workers indicate having participated in some form of training over a period of two years (Borghans, Fouarge and De Grip, 2011). Yet, the participation rates decrease sharply after workers turn 50; approximately 35 percent of 60 years old workers participate in training (Borghans *et al.*, 2011).

5.2. Theoretical background

Organisations are often defined as goal-oriented systems that strive toward profit maximization, continuity, and maintaining a healthy market position (Kalleberg *et al.*, 1996). Managers in organisations are supposed to contribute to these goals through, among other things, realization of high production levels and low costs, low absenteeism, good social relations and maintenance of useful sources of knowledge and contacts, and recruitment of qualified staff (Kalleberg *et al.*, 1996). Employees' skills and knowledge are among the most important assets of organisations, and updating and upgrading them is essential to maintain a competitive advantage (Torraco, 2000). Training of staff members may be an important instrument when updating skills and knowledge.

5.2.1. Individual characteristics
Managers' decisions to grant training opportunities to their workers may include evaluation of workers' various individual characteristics. There are two major theoretical perspectives on training and individual characteristics that affect this process. These different perspectives on training, as an investment or as a reward, lead to different predictions as to which individuals will be offered training. Both perspectives will be elaborated on below.

Human capital theory presents an economic approach to training. It analyzes investments in human capital and rates of return of education and training (Becker, 1975). Human capital theory predicts that skills and knowledge are likely to become obsolete over the life course, stressing the importance of lifetime investments in human capital. Training is a measure that improves workers' skills and enhances productivity, and is offered when the future benefits of the investments exceed direct and indirect cost of training. In line with this theory, organisations will invest in skills-updating programs to prevent skills obsolescence and will profit from higher employee productivity.

This approach to training focuses on the factors that can limit productivity decline or increase returns to training investments. Companies are more likely to offer training that is specific rather than general. While specific training is primarily useful at the company that offers it, general training can also be applied at other companies. Participation in general training may increase the risk of employee turnover and loss of the investment (Acemoglu and Pischke, 1999; Bishop, 1997).

Social exchange theory underscores the importance of an exchange in the social situation and its consequences. One of its basic assumptions is that individuals form social exchange relationships with others when interacting. Reciprocity rules govern such exchanges, which involve both social and economic outcomes (*i.e.*, esteem and financial resources, respectively) (Cropanzano and Mitchell, 2005; Molm, 1994). Social exchange thus comprises actions that are contingent on the rewarding reactions of others, which over time provide for mutually rewarding relationships. From that perspective on training, both managers and employees possess resources that can be exchanged over the course of the employment history (Balkin and Richebé, 2007).

As both theories put forward different objectives of training, the factors that contribute to training opportunities will also differ. The major contrast refers to the evaluation of workers' performance. Skill obsolescence is particularly likely to affect older workers, as they have experienced a high pace of technological change in the course of their careers. Various studies show that employers perceive obsolete skills to go hand-in-hand with lower productivity (Remery *et al.*, 2003; Taylor and Walker, 1994). In line with human capital theory, workers are rewarded proportionally to their productivity (Becker, 1975; Martin and Harder, 1994). Yet, while employers observe the discrepancy between the productivity of their employees and the wages they receive; they have limited possibility adjusting the wages accordingly (Conen *et al.*, 2012). Investments in lifelong learning are assumed to be the most beneficial solution to that problem as it helps closing that wage-productivity gap. Skills-updating will be especially important for workers who perform poorly; their training will be necessary bringing older workers' performance up to organisational standards for their position or retraining them to taking a different, possibly less demanding position. Reasoning from social exchange theory might lead to a different hypothesis. Good performance is one such resource that older workers can offer, as workers who perform well are a valuable asset to an organisation, their productivity aligns organisational expectations and they contribute effectively to organisational goals. Therefore, managers will use training as a reward for their older workers' good performance. Hence while human capital theory predicts that training opportunities will be primarily offered to workers whose productivity is low and/or falling short of organisational standards, social exchange theory leads to the opposite prediction, stressing that it is highly productive workers who will get trained.

Performance is however not the only aspect that will be evaluated. Human capital theory suggests that age also plays an important role in determining older workers' training. Different studies have shown that older workers are less likely to be offered training (see Bishop, 1997). In line with human capital theory, the direct and indirect costs of training are compared with the discounted future benefits of the human capital investment (Davies and Elias, 2004). The lack of involvement in training older workers thus arises because of the limited period over which employers might reap a return to their investment.

Human capital theory predicts that investment in training will also be affected by older workers' health status. Mental strain is one of the main reasons for employee exit from the labor force (Statistics Netherlands, 2012). Both physical and mental health issues increase the risk of productivity loss and absenteeism, lowering the prospects of returns to the training investments, and can thus lead to larger turnover of older workers. In the human capital approach to training, managers might be less likely to offer training opportunities to workers with frail health, in order to limit the risk of investment loss.

Social exchange theory stresses the importance of resources exchanged in the course of the employment history. Next to satisfactory performance, older workers can also contribute their positive work attitude to this exchange. A good work attitude signals professional motivation that contributes more effectively to organisational goals. This motivation has been described as "the willingness to exert high levels of effort towards organisational goals" (Robbins, 1993, p. 205). Motivation is the resource that has a long-term, positive effect on worker performance within an organisation and contributes to higher productivity, organisational commitment and lower turnover risk (Mathieu and Zajac, 1990). In return, organisations will reward this positive work attitude of older workers by granting training opportunities.

These two theoretical perspectives on training thus lead to different hypotheses on the impact of individual characteristics of older workers on training opportunities. Based on human capital theory, we predict that *managers will be more likely to offer training opportunities to older workers whose performance is moderate* (Hypothesis 1), *who are younger* (Hypothesis 2) *and who enjoy good mental and physical health* (Hypothesis 3). In line with social exchange theory, we predict *managers will be more likely to offer training to workers who perform well* (Hypothesis 4). Moreover, *workers' positive work attitude will have a positive effect on managers offering training opportunities* (Hypothesis 5).

5.2.2.   Managers' characteristics

In their training choices managers may also be affected by normative age and workers' participation in the labor force. Social norms are customary rules of behavior that coordinate human interactions and affect decisions (Coleman, 1990; Etzioni, 2000). In the current study we focused on perceived age norms regarding employment transitions (Settersten and Hagestad, 1996). As indicated by Van Solinge and Henkens (2007), retirement age norms illustrate the appropriate time to retire, and they affect retirement decisions of older workers. Previous chapters have shown that age norms held by managers do affect their hiring and retention decisions regarding older workers, and form a barrier to prolonged employment. Similarly, managers' age norms toward older workers' retirement are assumed to affect their offering of training opportunities for older workers. Higher age norms with respect to retirement imply a more positive attitude toward older workers and their labor market participation. This more positive outlook will also increase support for older workers' training and decrease discrimination of that group. In addition, managers that are more positive about employment at older ages will view training of older workers as a justified investment with probable positive returns. We therefore predict that *the higher the norms held by managers with respect to labor market participation of older workers, the more likely they are to offer training opportunities to them* (Hypothesis 6).

5.2.3.   Training characteristics

Offering training opportunities is presumably affected by the consideration of costs involved and the aim of training. As direct supervisors of workers, managers might be more likely to offer training that is aimed at increasing skills in a worker's current position than in a different one. There is evidence suggesting that managers recommend training based on its utility for daily-performance tasks (Bishop, 1997). Offering training that targets several skills applicable in a different position will benefit the worker and the broader organisation but another department will then recoup the return to that investment. With respect to costs involved, we assume that managers will be more likely to offer older workers training that involves lower costs. We therefore predict that *managers will be more likely to offer training opportunities when training aims at updating skills for the position workers occupy than for another position in an organisation* (Hypothesis 7), and that *managers will be more likely to offer training opportunities when training is free of charge than when it costs a month's salary* (Hypothesis 8).

5.3.   Data and methods

To answer the research questions a survey and four vignette experiments on training opportunities for older workers were developed. I collected the data by accessing the sample of the Longitudinal Internet Studies for the Social Sciences of Tilburg University (http://www.lissdata.nl/lissdata/). All individuals were selected based on a true probability sample of households drawn from the population register by Statistics Netherlands. The data was collected in April/May 2010.

5.3.1.   Study
During a survey background information on managers was collected and a month later vignette experiments were conducted. A vignette experiment is a method intended for the investigation of decisions. The basic item of the survey is a vignette, which is a short description of a situation or a person, generated by combining characteristics randomly manipulated by the researcher (Ganong and Coleman, 2006; Wallander, 2009). The four experiments differed with respect to *the aim of training and time and cost* involved in the training. For the *aim of training*, two options were applied: training targeted at 1) updating skills in the worker's current position, or at 2) acquiring skills for a different position in the same organisation. For those training options two *cost* schemes were further differentiated: a) training that took two days and cost a month's salary, or b) training that took ten days and was free of charge. This approach allows us to estimate managers' propensity to offer training opportunities across different types of training.

5.3.2.   Participants
This study was directed at managers. In the LISS panel they were identified based on the questions: *What is your current occupation?* and *Do you supervise others?* The total sample of managers who participated in this study amounted to 153. All respondents were responsible in their daily routines for employment decisions regarding their subordinates. The sample consisted of 117 males and 36 females, and the mean age of respondents was 45.7 (range 24-65, SD=9.6). *Table 5.1* presents the descriptive statistics.

Table 5.1. Descriptive statistics, N=153

	N total	Min	Max	Mean/ %	St. Dev.
Dependent variable pooled analysis					
Training desirability	765	1	11	4.84	2.47
Dependent variable per experiment					
Training desirability (exp 1a: own position, 2 days, cost month's salary)	200	1	11	4.48	2.34
Training desirability (exp 1b: own position, 10 days, free of charge)	220	1	11	5.29	2.51
Training desirability (exp 2a: different position, 2 days, cost month's salary)	170	1	11	4.82	2.37
Training desirability (exp 2b: different position, 10 days, free of charge)	175	1	11	4.69	2.51
Training characteristics					
Cost of training	765	0	1	48.05	
Goal of training	765	0	1	54.55	
Characteristics of respondents					
Managerial position	153				
Higher supervisory positions		0	1	44.1	
Intermediate supervisory or commercial positions		0	1	40.9	
Supervisory manual workers		0	1	14.9	
Age (years)	153	24	65	45.7	9.6
Male	153	0	1	76.6	
Education (years)	153	8	18	15.2	2.35
Job level of subordinates	153				
Low-skilled		0	1	18.9	
High-skilled		0	1	81.1	
Size of organisation	153	10	10,000	445.8	1,228.5
Sector	153				
Industry		0	1	33.7	
Services		0	1	38.9	
Public		0	1	27.7	
Age norm	153	50	80	63.9	6.20

Source: LISS panel study.

In vignette experiments respondents judge only a random selection from the vignette universe (Wallander, 2009). In our study, each participant was randomly assigned to one of the four experimental conditions and received a random sample of 5 vignettes that corresponded to that experiment.

5.3.3.   Measurements
Vignettes
In this study various hypothetical older workers were described with several characteristics and the training situation was placed in a specific organisational context. In the set up managers were presented with vignettes where instruction explicitly mentioned that all workers were highly motivated to participate in training. Presumably, older workers are often unwilling to participate in training, which is an often-mentioned reason behind their low training participation (Armstrong-Stassen and Templer, 2005; Cully *et al.*, 2001; Taylor, 2006). Focusing only on motivated older workers helps distinguish managers' preferences with respect to training opportunities without the confounding effect of these workers' assumed lack of motivation. The four experimental conditions differed with respect to goal of training and its costs (2x2). The instructions applied in each experiment are presented below:

1a) The employee described below wishes to follow a 2-day external training (cost of a month salary, paid by the employer) that is related to his position. What is the chance that you would offer this training opportunity?

1b) The employee described below wishes to follow a 10-time 2-day external training that is related to his position. The training is free of charge. What is the chance that you would offer this training opportunity?

2a) The employee described below wishes to follow a 2-day external training (cost of a month salary, paid by the employer) that is related to another position in your company. What is the chance that you would offer this training opportunity?

2b) The employee described below wishes to follow a 10-time 2-day external training that is related to another position in your company. The training is free of charge. What is the chance that you would offer this training opportunity?

Each manager rated each vignette on an 11-point scale, ranging from 1 (absolutely would not offer training opportunity) to 11 (absolutely would not offer training opportunity). *Figure 5.1* depicts an example of a vignette used in Experiment 1a.

Figure 5.1. Example of a vignette applied in Experiment 1a

An employee described below wishes to follow a 2-day external training (costs a month's salary, paid by an employer) that is related to his function. What is the chance that you would accept this wish?

Context:

Financial situation	Stable
Employee	
Age	62
Gender	Male
Physical health	Good
Mental health	Limited
Scope of the work week	3 days a week
Performance	Moderate
Work attitude	Positive

What is the likelihood that you would support that wish and recommend training?

1	2	3	4	5	6	7	8	9	10	11

Absolutely would not offer training opportunity   Neutral   Absolutely would offer training opportunity

Although each experiment referred to a different type of training, all vignettes consisted of the same variables and their respective levels. The eight vignette characteristics were: *financial situation of the organisation* (solid/moderate); *physical health condition* (good/not very good); *mental health condition* (good/limited); *work scope* (works 5 days a week/works 3 days a week); *older worker's performance* (very good, good, moderate) and *older worker's work attitude* (positive/negative). In the vignettes we also included *older worker's age* (50, 54, 58, 62 and 66) and *workers' gender* (male/female). Given all possible combinations of the variables and their respective levels, a universe of 960 unique vignettes was created (*i.e.* 2x2x2x2x3x2x5x2; for details see *table 5.2*). Variables measured in vignette experiments were included in the analysis as dummy variables. Except for the variable *performance*, where a new dummy was constructed that combined the answers 'good' and 'very good' into one category, all other dummy variables represent the level of each factor.

Table 5.2. Organisational contexts and employee attributes in the vignette

Item	Categories
Organisation	
Financial position of the organisation	Solid
	Moderate
Employee	
Age	50
	54
	58
	62
	66
Gender	Male
	Female
Physical health	Good
	Not very good
Mental health	Good
	Limited
Scope of the work week	5 days a week
	3 days a week
Performance	Very good
	Good
	Moderate
Work attitude	Positive
	Negative

Source: LISS panel study.

Survey

A month before the experiments were conducted, questions on age norms and background characteristics of managers were collected. Existing age norms are measured on the basis of the open question: *At what age do you consider a person too old to work in your organisation for 20 hours a week or more?* This question was previously posed in a representative survey of European employers (Henkens and Van Dalen, 2012). The answer ranged from 40 to 100. The mean of the age in the total sample was 63.9 years with an SD of 6.2. Modal value of age was 65 — approximately 32 percent of respondents indicated that the retirement age of 65 is when a person is too old to work 20 hours or more.

In the analysis we controlled for *organisation's financial position*, as investing in older workers' skill-updating programs will be advocated if organisations can accommodate additional expenditures. This variable was included in vignettes. Sector of the organisation was based on the question: *In which sector is your company operating?* Following the European Commission division of sectors, three categories were constructed: *Industry, services and public.* During this study the control variables *respondents' gender* and *respondents' age* were also collected.

5.3.4. Analyses

In a vignette design, the unit of analysis is the vignette (Ganong and Coleman, 2006). As each manager in his respective experiments judged five vignettes, our data have a hierarchical structure by design, therefore observations are not independent (Wallander, 2009). Multilevel models were applied to deal with the hierarchical structure of the data (Hox, 2002). Fixed models on the data pooled from all four experiments and a survey were estimated. Specifically, level-2 predictors included in each model regarded managers (managers' age norms and their demographic characteristics, sector of the organisation and type of training) and level-1 variables consisted of individual attributes of older workers that were included in the vignettes.

In the analysis we evaluated factors that affect managers' propensity to offer training opportunities to older workers. Three models were estimated. Model 1 was aimed at decomposing the total variance between the two levels of analysis, without considering the potential predictors at each level. In Model 2 we tested our hypotheses on the impact of characteristics of older workers on training opportunities. Model 3 included characteristics of managers and organisations in the assessment of training opportunities as level-2 predictors. In this model we also included the dummy variables representing different trainings to test whether training types affected managers' offerings of training opportunities. The variable cost denoted training that amounted to a month's salary and took two days (reference category was training that was free of charge and took 10 days to complete). The variable goal referred to the purpose of training and denoted training aimed at increasing qualification in the same position (reference category was training aimed at increasing skills for a different position in the same organisation).

5.4. Results

Table 3 presents the results of the analyses. Model 1 contains only fixed and random effects of the intercept. Based on this model we can deduce whether the training opportunities scores differed between managers and different types of training. Intraclass correlation shows that this level accounts for 40.4 percent of the total variance in training scores. The intercept illustrates that on average training opportunities were evaluated rather low, at 4.48 (on a scale running from 1 to 11). This implies that managers do not generally favor offering training to older workers.

Model 2 includes individual characteristics of workers. Based on human capital theory we hypothesized those workers' poor performance will result in more training opportunities (Hypothesis 1). Also, we predicted that training opportunities would decrease with worker's age (Hypothesis 2) and workers' poor health condition (Hypothesis 3). The results show that training opportunities decrease significantly with workers' age; workers who are 62 and 66 years old were less likely to be offered the chance to follow training. Also, poor physical and mental health decreased the participation chances. Another central question is how older workers' performance is related to training opportunities. The results show that poor work performance does not lead to higher chances of receiving training opportunities, which contradicts the human capital theory hypothesis (Hypothesis 1). On the contrary, we observe that workers who perform very well were more likely to be granted training opportunities, which lends support to the hypothesis based on social exchange theory (Hypothesis 4). Also, in line with Hypothesis 5, positive work attitudes enhanced managers' propensity to offer training opportunities. In our study we also controlled for workers' gender and the scope of the contract. Full-time employees were more likely to be offered training. No difference was found in how training opportunities were offered to male or female employees.

In Model 3 characteristics of managers and the organisation were added to the model. None of the effects of individual characteristics of older workers previously included in the model changed substantially. We observe that in organisations that enjoyed a solid financial situation managers were more likely to offer training opportunities to their older staff members. Training opportunities were lower in both the industry and service sectors compared to the public sector. Neither age norms nor managers' gender has a significant effect on their training opportunities. Yet, the likelihood of offering training opportunities to older workers decreased with managers' age.

In this study we also aimed at distinguishing between the training opportunities in different training types; training aimed at upgrading skills applicable in the position that workers occupy and also training targeting internal mobility of older workers. Also different cost schemes were included in the design. The results in the last column of *table 5.3* show that managers' decisions did not differ across training aimed at different positions or at cost involved in training. Also, we have investigated if those training schemes were applied differently in particular conditions. To this end we introduced several interaction terms between type of training and characteristics of older workers (results not shown). None of the interaction terms were significant. In the consecutive analyses we have also tested for the random effects of the individual-level variables, *i.e.* whether the effects of specific individual predictors differed across managers (results not shown). The analyses revealed that there was significant variability in how managers considered training opportunities for the oldest workers (workers at the age of 66), workers' work attitude and their physical health. We studied additional models with cross-level interactions to account for those differences. None of the introduced cross-level interactions was found to explain the variability of age and work attitude across managers. In the analysis of random slope of health we found that managers, who held higher age norms, attached less value to good physical health condition of older workers.

5.5. Discussion and conclusions

Although training of older workers is often seen as key practice to increase labor market participation of older workers (OECD, 2006), there is only limited insight into what factors affect managers' decisions regarding training opportunities for older workers. This is surprising, given the fact that managers are the gate keepers when it comes to offering training to their staff; they carry the responsibility for employability of their personnel and define training opportunities. The study is the first to analyze training opportunities for older workers among managers. In the analysis we contrasted predictions stemming from human capital theory have been contrasted with hypotheses based on social exchange theory. Four vignette experiments were designed to answer the research question. The data was collected among a sample of 153 managers in various Dutch organisations and multilevel models were estimated.

Human capital theory predicts that managers are more likely to offer training when they expect higher returns to the investment or when they intend to lower the risk of productivity decline due to skills deterioration. In line with this hypothesis, workers closer to their retirement and less healthy have fewer training opportunities. Training opportunities clearly decreased with

Table 5.3. Results of the multilevel model

	Model 1		Model 2		Model 3	
	Coef.	t-score	Coef.	t-score	Coef.	t-score
Fixed effects						
Employee's characteristics						
Worker's age						
50 years old (ref.)			—		—	
54 years old			-0,15	-0,77	-0,14	-0,76
58 years old			-0,05	-0,26	-0,08	-0,41
62 years old			-0,52**	-2,66	-0,53**	-2,72
66 years old			-1,35***	-7,11	-1,35***	-7,17
Physical health good (ref. not good)			0,61***	5,00	0,61***	4,96
Mental health good (ref. limited)			0,42***	3,46	0,46***	3,48
Performance						
Moderate			-0,71***	-5,48	-0,71***	-5,41
Very good or good			—		—	
Work attitude						
Positive			1,66***	13,47	1,65***	13,50
Negative			—	--	—	
Male (ref. female)			0,05	0,36	0,05	0,45
Work scope						
5 days a week			0,45***	3,58	0,49***	3,91
3 days a week (ref.)			—		—	

	Model 1 B	Model 1 t	Model 2 B	Model 2 t	Model 3 B	Model 3 t
Organisation's characteristic						
Financial situation-						
Solid					0,33*	2,45
Moderated (ref.)					—	
Sector						
Industry					-0,90*	-2,61
Services					-0,94**	-2,76
Public (ref.)						
Manager's characteristics						
Age norm					0,03	1,45
Male					0,30	0,91
Manager's age					-0,03*	-2,34
Training cost and form						
Cost a month salary					-0,31	-1,12
Free of charge (ref.)					—	
Oriented on own position					0,19	0,72
Oriented at different position (ref.)					—	
Constant	4,84***	33,38	3,94***	16,67	3,65***	2,22
Random effects						
Variance level 2	2,48 (0,37)		2,57 (0,35)		2,24 (0,31)	
Variance level 1	3,65 (0,20)		2,35 (0,13)		2,33 (0,13)	
Model fit - Deviance (df)	3388,84 (3)		3111,02 (13)		3087,94 (21)	
N of vignettes (N of respondents)	765 (153)		765 (153)		765 (153)	

Notes: In parentheses: standard error for variance components, * p<0.05; ** p<0.01; *** p<0.001.
Source: LISS panel study.

age, and the impact of poor health also followed an expected pattern. This study shows that older workers who perform well and are characterized by a positive work attitude have more training opportunities, which lends support to the hypothesis derived from social exchange theory.

Workers who are not performing well are much more likely to be excluded from training. This might be an indication that managers do not take responsibility for the development of such workers and may be interpreted as a form of disengagement on the part of supervisors. Combined with the evidence from research by Damman, Henkens and Kalmijn (2013) on older workers' disengagement prior to retirement, our findings thus suggest that the process of work disengagement takes place among both older workers and their managers.

We have examined in more detail training opportunities for different types of training and costs involved than is usually the case. Next to specific training aimed at the worker's current position we have also looked at general training targeted at skills acquisition for internal mobility. Contrary to our expectations, no significant differences were found for either training aim or cost involved. Clearly, in their evaluation of training opportunities for older workers managers focus on aspects other than the specific aim and cost of training. Future research should evaluate if training opportunities are dependent on the content of training.

Surprisingly, age norms held by managers did not affect their evaluation of training opportunities for older workers. Earlier chapters have shown that perception of limits for employment influence managers' judgment of retention and hiring of older workers. Evaluation of training opportunities clearly differs from the other decisions; managers do not weigh the rationale of employment but deal with development of their staff, and their evaluation is based on factors other than their perception of employment deadlines of older workers.

Although upgrading skills is an investment that benefits both workers who participate in training and the organisation that employs them, costs of employer-provided training are usually compensated by organisations. We show that training investments are dependent on the organisation's financial situation, which is not surprising given the current financial crisis. We found strong support for the notion that organisations that have been recently affected by crisis reduce their training investments (Barrett and O'Connell, 2001).

We conclude with some methodological remarks. We designed four vignette experiments to look at various training forms for older workers. By designing experiments that regard each of the conditions separately, we ensure the quality of the data. Had type of training and cost been included as factors in vignettes, a random selection of vignettes might have resulted in lower representation of certain conditions in the final sample. We perceive this distinction as a noteworthy strength of our study. One has to keep in mind, however, that we asked managers to assess hypothetical situations. In real-life training situations managers may act or decide differently. Yet, the respondents were managers employed in organisations and not students, as is often the case in experimental studies (Barr and Hitt, 1986). Consequently, the results of the study are more generalizable than earlier studies on employment decisions.

Despite those limitations, this study adds to the long-standing debate in the field of human resources management on relations between training and productivity of older workers. Our findings contradict the assumption that training is offered by managers to those workers who might need it the most (OECD, 2006). The political rhetoric on the importance of lifelong learning and recommendations that follow (CEC (Commission of the European Communities), 2000; Organisation for Economic Co-operation and Development (OECD), 2003) do not reflect the complexity of the decision-making processes that take place in the organisations. What is the least sure is that those workers who need the training the most are the ones to be offered it.

6. Conclusions

6.1. Background and the aim of the study

Prolonged and productive employment of older workers is a necessary condition to maintain welfare and social security systems threatened by ageing populations (OECD, 2006). Despite this importance, the labour market position of older workers is much worse than that of workers in primal age (Conen, Henkens and Schippers, 2011). As the retirement process has become a more gradual transition from a working to a non-working life, different employment options, like early exit, temporary return to the labour force or bridge employment, are available for older workers (Henkens, Van Solinge and Van Dalen, 2013; Hardy, 2002). Yet, not much is known about the factors that contribute to those different outcomes for older workers. The general aim of this dissertation was to gain more understanding of the dynamics in the labour market participation of older workers around retirement age in the Netherlands. In particular, the current study has evaluated which individual characteristics of older workers, organisations and managers affect managers' decisions to hire older workers, offer them training opportunities and retain them in organisations. After all, it is managers are in charge and decide whether older workers' plans and desires to stay in or regain employment will be realised.

Moreover, this study also assessed empirically the potential role of managers' attitudes on their behaviour regarding hiring, training and retention of older workers. The analyses took into account two aspects of the mental system of managers, namely their stereotypical views of older workers' productivity and managers' age norms with respect to appropriate timing of exit from the labour force. This study contributes to a better understanding of how attitudes affect employment decision-making.

To evaluate the decisions that managers take and the impact of attitudes on those decisions, this dissertation utilises two data sources. First, a pilot study consisting of vignette experiments was conducted. A vignette is a short description of a situation or a person generated by combining characteristics randomly manipulated by the researcher (Ganong and Coleman, 2006; Wallander, 2009). By presenting respondents with concrete and detailed descriptions of the situation of a person, this approach offers the possibility to study how context and different conditions affect people's judgments (Wallander, 2009). The data was collected among managers during a focus group meeting at the Netherlands Interdisciplinary Demographic Institute (NIDI) (see Van Dalen *et al.*, 2009) and among business students of Utrecht University. Chapter 2 drew on the data collected in this pilot.

After this pilot, the major study was conducted. This study combined a survey and vignette experiments. By accessing the sample of the LISS panel (Longitudinal Internet Studies for the Social Sciences of Tilburg University) a sample of managers was approached. The data was collected in two stages: First a survey was administered to managers and questions about the characteristics of respondents, their age norms and stereotypes were posed. One month later the same managers were approached again to complete a vignette study. In this research design I followed the recommendation put forward by Liefbroer and Billari (2010) who suggest that to properly analyse the effect of norms on behaviour, the perception of norms needs to be observed before the actual behaviour. The same applies to stereotypes. This study aimed at measuring those attitudes before the experimental studies, with a sufficient time span between the studies to limit the risk of carry over effects (Leeuw *et al.*, 2006). This semi-panel design is well suited to analyze the effect of stereotypes and norms on (hypothetical) behaviour. Chapters 3, 4 and 5 drew on this data. In the following sections the results of the analyses are summarised.

6.2. Summary of the results and conclusions from the empirical chapters

6.2.1. *Hiring of early retirees*
Chapters 2 and 3 both dealt with the hiring of early retirees. The main research question addressed in Chapter 2 was: *What factors influence managers' decisions concerning the reemployment of early retirees?* This study took an initial step towards gaining more insight into the factors that affect hiring of early retirees and used data that was collected during a pilot study held during a focus group meeting and among business students of Utrecht University. This study consisted only of vignette study. In total 20 managers and 17 students evaluated 12 vignettes each.

In this study I tested hypotheses regarding the impact of organisational as well as individual characteristics of older workers on their chances to re-enter labour market. The results show that, in line with the hypothesis, the hiring of early retirees was most likely to occur when organisations faced structural or, to a lesser extent, incidental labour force shortages. This study also focused on how individual characteristics of early retirees (such as their human capital, health status or age) affected their hiring chances. To illustrate the impact of various characteristics, early retirees were differentiated with respect to their employability, *i.e.* the ability to maintain or regain employment (Fugate, Kinicki and Ashforth, 2004). Early retirees were described as 'highly', 'moderately' or 'low' employable. A retiree with *high employability* was identified as an applicant who had experience in a similar position, retired a month ago, was healthy, was 58 years old, and had sent an unsolicited application. *Moderate employability* referred to an applicant who had experience in a similar position, retired no more than half-a-year ago, was healthy, was 62 years old, and had sent an unsolicited application. *Low employability* described an applicant who did not have experience in a similar position, retired at least one-and-a-half years ago, was healthy, was 65 years old, and had sent an unsolicited application.

For each of these categories the hiring desirability scores were estimated for different organisational circumstances. In general, the hiring of retirees had a low priority for managers. Even under the most beneficial conditions, if we consider a retiree with all characteristics in favour of re-employment (*e.g.* highly employable), in an organisation facing structural labour-force shortages, the overall score was 6.6 on a scale from 1 (hiring very undesirable) to 11 (hiring very desirable). This score has almost a neutral value — if anything, managers were indifferent about hiring early retirees. For each retiree whose profile differed and was less favourable, the scores representing the desirability for hiring dropped. The lowest score was obtained by those applicants with low employability (score of 3.0 in an organisation that is in need for new staff members). This suggest that re-entry of those early retirees becomes undesirable or very undesirable, despite the organisational labour force shortages.

These results suggest that early retirees are not welcomed with open arms by employing organisations and in the best-case scenario managers are only slightly positive about hiring them. Although more diverse paths towards retirement are possible for older workers, access to those trajectories is greatly dependent on managers' support. The results of this study indicate that manages hinder these dynamics by restricting the re-employment of people who are around retirement age.

This study also compared students' and managers' hiring practices and decisions. Employing students as surrogate in studies on the managerial decision-making process often raised the question of the generalisability of those studies (see Barr and Hitt, 1996). As students miss hands-on experience, they would not be able to evaluate the context of the decisions as more experienced managers do. The results of this chapter show that fairly consistent scores were given by both groups of respondents and that they only differed in how they evaluated early retirees' health status. While both managers and students perceived this factor to be an important aspect of early retirees re-entry into the labour force, students assigned significantly higher values to this characteristic. This suggests that students, although similar in their evaluations to managers, are more susceptible to evaluate the most obvious factors.

Chapter 3 replicated the results of the study presented in Chapter 2 and extended the analysis by looking at the impact of managers' attitudes towards older workers on the hiring of early retirees. Many studies describe that attitudes are one of the forces behind unfavorable employment outcomes for older workers (Finkelstein and Burke, 1998; Taylor, 2008). In this chapter attitudes towards older workers are defined as age norms about the timing of labour market exit, *i.e.* when a person is too old to work for an organisation for at least 20 hours a week. Next to age norms, managers' stereotypes regarding older workers' productivity were also taken into account. The research question posed in this study was: *How do ageist stereotypes and age norms, next to attributes of applicants, affect managers' propensity to hire early retirees?*

The analyses in this study were conducted with the data that was collected by accessing a sample of the LISS panel, and consisted of a survey and a vignette study. The profiles of early retirees presented in the vignettes included in Chapter 3 differed only slightly from the profiles applied in the earlier study, and also included gender of older workers and their social capital. Access to the LISS sample resulted in larger and a more representative sample of managers than for the pilot study. In total 238 managers participated in the study and each judged 5 vignettes. Multilevel models were estimated.

In this chapter the major focus lay on the impact of managers' attitudes towards older workers on managers' their decisions to hire early retirees. I hypothesised that more positive attitudes towards older workers will lead to more positive hiring decisions. More specifically, that higher age norms of labour market participation of older workers lead to more positive evaluations of early retirees who apply for a job. I also hypothesised that more positive perceptions of older workers' productivity, defined both in terms of soft skills (pro-social behaviour that is not job-specific but which is important for the broader organisational environment) and hard skills (mental and physical capacity, willingness to learn new skills and adapt to new technologies, and flexibility; see Van Dalen *et al.*, 2010b), will be associated with higher hiring chances for older workers.

The multilevel analyses confirmed that managers' hiring decisions were affected by their age norms as to when a person should be still working. Age norms indicated in the sample ranged from 40 to 100 and the average was 65 years. The impact of age norms clearly identifies the existence of 'time schedules' and supports the idea that social norms affect human actions (Coleman, 1990; Etzioni, 2000). Surprisingly, neither soft nor hard skill stereotypes affected managers' predisposition towards hiring early retirees.

The analyses revealed that the effect of age norms remains a significant predictor of hiring early retirees, even after controlling for characteristics of organisations and applicants. Also, the results for the individual and organisational factors were fairly consistent with the results reported in Chapter 2. To illustrate the importance of managers' age norms, hiring scores were estimated for each value of age norms. Here, similarly to Chapter 2, applicants were described in terms of their employability and two categories of applicants: the 'high' and the 'low' employable were distinguished. An early retiree with *high employability* was identified as an applicant with relevant experience, retired for a month, 58 years old and appearing energetic. An early retiree with *low employability* was described as an applicant, who did not have relevant experience, was retired for at least one-and-a-half year, was 65 years old and did not appear energetic. The effect of age norms on hiring likelihood scores for these two applicant categories was computed in two organisational situations: Structural labour force shortages and need for downsizing.

The results indicated that managers' age norms are important impediments for early retirees in the labour market. For a highly employable individual applying for a position in an organisation that is in need of new staff members, the hiring desirability score takes a value of approximately 6.7 (on a scale running from 1 to 11), which is the score for the lowest age norm – that is if a manager perceives age 50 as the limit of employment. This score is just above the neutral value of 6. A same-category applicant dealing with managers who consider the age deadline for employment to be 80 obtains scores approaching 8. When a highly employable applicant seeks a position in an organisation shedding jobs and when a manager holds age norms at the minimum level of 65, hiring scores peak above the neutral value of 6 and approach a value of 7. A similar effect of age norms is observed for low-employable applicants in both organisational conditions, although in those cases the hiring score does not exceed the neutral value of 6.

These findings thus show thus that age norms hamper a return to the labour force. Chances of early retirees in the labour market are lower at older ages, and managers are negatively preoccupied about hiring anyone beyond a certain age. Yet, organisational forces and the individual characteristics of applicants also affect the choices managers make. The results of this chapter confirm the importance of human capital for the employment chances of early retirees as applicants with relevant experience were more likely to be successful in their application process. Taken together, these results show that hiring of early retirees is a complex process and age norms are woven into the broader context of work relations.

6.2.2. Retention of older workers

Chapter 4 focused on factors affecting managers' decisions to retain older workers. Among others, the impact of managers' attitudes towards older workers on managers' decisions was also evaluated. The research question posed in this study read as follows: *How do ageist stereotypes and age norms, next to attributes of applicants, affect managers' propensity to retain their older workers?* This study drew on data collected through the LISS panel survey. Multilevel models were estimated to test the hypotheses.

This dissertation evaluated factors affecting retention and thus deals with 'insiders' – current staff members whose strengths and weaknesses managers were able to evaluate during the employment history. I argue that dealing with insiders lowers the uncertainty that is a part of the hiring process. Consequently, it may restrict application of general images that are assumed to lower the transaction costs when external applicants are hired (Phelps, 1972; Busch, Dahl and Dietrich, 2009; Van Dalen *et al.*, 2010b). Therefore, I expect that higher age norms and more positive evaluation of older workers productivity (in terms of soft and hard skills) will affect managers' decisions positively.

The results partly support this hypothesis and show that managers who perceive higher age limits for employment tend to be more positive towards retention of older workers for a few more years. Contrary to my hypothesis the perception of hard qualities of older workers did not affect managers' decisions. Finally, soft qualities were found to affect those choices positively:

managers who perceived older workers to possess soft skills more than younger workers were also more likely to support retention of older workers.

The analysis has shown that various other factors also contribute to managers' virtual retention decisions. To illustrate the importance of the different groups of explanatory variables, the retention scores were predicted for various market conditions and managers' norms about retirement age. Older workers were again defined in terms of their employability, *e.g.* the ability to secure and maintain employment (Fugate, Kinicki and Ashforth, 2004). In this study I defined workers with high employability as those whose experience was difficult to replace and who were versatile in their tasks, healthy, willing to participate in training and motivated to stay employed. Workers characterised by low employability lacked experience that was difficult to replace, and were not occupationally flexible, were in frail health, were unwilling to participate in training and looking forward to retirement. The results show that in the situation where organisations shed jobs and managers' age norm was low (*i.e.* 50 years), the predicted retention recommendation score for highly employable older workers was just above the neutral value – 6.3, on a scale from 1 (retention very undesirable) to 11 (retention very desirable). This score rose substantially to 8.2 when managers' age norm increased to 80. Retention chances of highly employable workers increased even further – to 9.3– when organisations faced labour- force shortages. These results stress the importance of employability of older workers, as this study demonstrates that low-employable workers have very limited chances of remaining employed even when the labour market conditions and the dispositions of managers are positive. Moreover, this study confirms that the employment opportunities for high-employable older workers largely extent dependent on labour market circumstances and existing age norms within organisations. The results suggest that although skills maintenance and lifelong learning are a key to older workers' labour force participation, the restrictions present in the labour market are crucial when retention is considered.

In this chapter I also explored whether decisions with respect to older workers differ for low and high-skilled workers. I hypothesised that retention chances of low- and high-skilled workers may be determined by different factors. Contrary to this expectation, the study revealed that managers evaluated various attributes similarly, regardless of the position level of their subordinates. This suggests that low- and high-skilled workers face the same type of restrictions in the labour force.

6.2.3.   Training opportunities for older workers
The final empirical chapter dealt with training opportunities for older workers. The research question posed in this study read as follows: *What are the factors that affect training opportunities for older workers?* This chapter evaluated the impact of individual characteristics of older workers, those of the organisation and also managers' perception of age norms on managers' propensity of offering older workers training opportunities. The analyses also were based on the data collected through the LISS panel survey on a sample of 153 managers in Dutch organisations. Multilevel models were estimated.

To study training opportunities for older workers, integrated two theoretical perspectives, namely human capital theory and social exchange theory. Human capital theory frames training as an investment in employees that benefits both the employee and the organisation (Becker, 1975). Social exchange theory instead frames training as a reward for worker performance (Cropanzano and Mitchell, 2005). I hypothesised that those two theories will differ in terms how managers evaluate the performance of older workers when offering them training opportunities. Based on human capital theory I hypothesised that low performance of older workers will lead to more training opportunities. Social exchange theory leads to the opposite prediction, stressing that it is highly productive workers who will get trained. Based on human capital theory,I also predicted that managers will be more likely to offer training opportunities to workers who are younger and in good mental and physical health. Following the logic of human capital theory, older workers are not worth the investment as the period during which organisation can profit from this investment is too short. In line with social exchange theory I hypothesised that managers will be more likely to offer training to workers who perform well and exhibit a positive work attitude.

The results show that managers were not very likely to offer training opportunities for older workers; the average training likelihood was 4.5 on a scale running from 1 (absolutely would not offer training opportunities) to 11 (absolutely would offer training opportunities). The results partly support human capital theory and indicate that workers closer to their retirement and less healthy will be offered fewer training opportunities. No effect of poor performance was found. On the other hand, this study shows that older workers who perform well and are characterised by a positive work attitude have more training opportunities, which lends support to the hypothesis derived from social exchange theory. In sum, workers who are not performing well are much more likely to be excluded from training. This suggests that managers do not take responsibility for the development of such workers, and that supervisors disengage from their less productive older workers in pre-retirement years. This finding contradicts the rhetoric on the importance of lifelong learning (*i.e.* OECD, 2003) as it shows that within organisations it is not at all certain that those workers who need training the most are also the ones to most likely receive it.

In this study I also assumed that training opportunities for older workers would be affected by managers' age norms. Higher age norms with respect to retirement timing imply a more positive attitude towards older workers and their employment. Managers who are more positive about employment at older ages will view the training of older workers as a justified investment with probable positive returns and therefore will be more likely to offer older workers training opportunities. Contrary to findings from earlier chapters, no support was found for the hypothesis that age norms affect managers' decisions with respect to offering training opportunities.

This study also examined managers' propensity to offer older workers different types of training. Most studies that focus on training report information on formal and specific training, *i.e.* training that can be applied only at the company that provides it (Becker, 1975; Leuven and Oosterbeek, 1999). Yet, less is known about different types of training and whether those differences affect managers' propensity to offer such opportunities to older workers. The conditions investigated include training aimed at upgrading skills applicable in the position that workers currently occupy, as well as training targeting internal mobility of older workers. Costs of training were also differentiated (training was either free of charge or cost a month salary). Contrary to my expectations, the results revealed that managers' decisions did not differ across types of training nor were related to different costs.

6.3.   Discussion and scientific relevance

6.3.1.   *Age norms*
The results of this dissertation show that managers' opinion on age norms affect their decisions to hire and retain older workers. As indicated by life-course scholars, there are informal expectations as to when behaviour should occur (Settersten, 1998), and such norms exert significant influence on life-transition behaviour (Settersten and Hagestad, 1996; Van Solinge and Henkens, 2007). These findings thus lend support to this notion, and

corroborate the link between social norms and human actions suggested by many theorists (Coleman, 1990; Etzioni, 2000).

In the case of hiring and retention those age norms prove to be an important predictor of managers' decisions. Although this relationship was positive, managers' decisions regarding hiring and retention of early retirees do not necessarily raise confidence in the improvement of the latter's labour market position. The overall hiring and retention scores were low. Moreover, most of the managers in this sample were convinced that the age deadline for work was 65 or younger. This suggests that although managerial norms can exert positive effects on hiring and retention behaviour, there is still little support for employment of workers in their late sixties.

I also evaluated the relation between managers' age norms and their offering training opportunities to older workers. The analyses revealed that managers' training decisions were not guided by their perceptions of employment timetables. These results point towards an idea that evaluations of training opportunities might differ from the decisions on hiring and retaining older workers. Managers do not weigh the rationale of employment but deal with development of their staff. Consequently, their evaluations might be based on aspects other than their perception of employment desirability at older ages.

6.3.2.   Stereotypes
This dissertation is among the first to test empirically the impact of ageist stereotypes on decisions that managers take with respect to older workers. There is a vast body of literature that suggests that ageist stereotypes are the mechanism behind low participation of older workers in the labour force and discriminatory behaviours against them (Chiu *et al.*, 2001; Finkelstein and Burke, 1998; Loretto *et al.*, 2000). Surprisingly, very limited support was found for the presence of stereotypes in such employment decisions. This dissertation shows that this aspect is less important when employment decisions regarding older workers are taken. Despite the fact that this study found only limited support for the presence of ageist stereotypes in the management of older workers, this does not mean that age stereotypes do not have an effect on decisions that managers take. Chui *et al.* (2001) showed that stereotypes affect managers' attitudes towards employment outcomes for older workers. Future research should replicate this study on a different sample of respondents, to determine if age stereotypes affect also behaviours.

Social psychologists assume that stereotypes form a cognitive mechanism or perceptual process that lead to behaviours. Yet, behaviour does not occur as simple reaction to the activated stereotypes. As put forward by Fazio (1990), the link between attitude and behaviour is not always consistent and depends on the individual definition of the situation an one enters. In his conceptual model a definition of the situation can be affected by perception of norms, *i.e.* appropriate courses of action in a given situation (Fazio, 1990). Fazio suggests that when attitudes do not align with norms, individuals are more likely to abide by normative expectations and act accordingly. In the context of the current study, the perception of when a person should exit the labour force might have affected a respondent's perception of the situation and overridden negative attitudes towards older workers. This suggests that negative perceptions of older workers' productivity were less influential than normative perceptions of timing of labour force exit.

This complex relationship between age norms and stereotypes and their impact on behaviour is further confirmed by the results of this study; the analyses revealed that although stereotypes and age norms represent general attitudes towards older workers, there is only a very weak link between them. In other words, age norms regarding retirement transitions may not be simple representations of older workers' perceived productivity. This suggests that the decision making process is indeed based on complex deliberations.

Given that norms exert great impact on behaviour, it is surprising that so far not much is known about the factors that affect norms regarding retirement transitions. Henkens (2010) suggested that age norms might change over time due to changing circumstances and institutional arrangements. To what extent age norms are culturally determined scripts and influenced by the formal age boundaries established by public and private pension schemes, or does the organisational age structure or organisational culture also affects them, is less clear. Van Dalen *et al.* (2012) have attempted to disentangle factors that affect age norms of managers in the Netherlands and several European countries, and shown that age norms are strongly associated with managers own retirement plans; the later managers themselves want to retire, the higher the normative retirement age. Yet, a greater focus on the factors that affect those timetables and on the real nature of general attitudes constitutes an interesting path for further inquiry.

6.3.3.   *Employment decisions*
This dissertation aimed at disentangling determinants of hiring, retention and training opportunities for older workers. This focus offers a comprehensive

view of the factors that affect different aspect of older workers participation in the labour force. In the current study for each of the decisions that managers took, outcomes for older workers were compared within this worker category and were not compared to other groups present in the labour force. This approach offered more insights into factors that affect hiring, retention and training opportunities for older workers yet does not show how older workers position themselves among younger applicants or potential training participants. It is possible that the employment chances of highly employable older workers are overvalued; in situations where highly employable workers of different age categories apply for jobs, managers may prefer those who are younger and equally qualified. To overcome this limitation, a future study could focus on a more age-diverse pool of workers that are subject to such decisions. That might increase the realism of the situation dedicted and offer more insight into older workers chances for retention, hiring or being offered training opportunities than could be given in this dissertation.

Older workers form a diverse group and one aspect that differentiates them is their employment status. To gain more insight into employment dynamics and older workers' chances of re-entering or changing employment, a focus on different categories of older applicants is necessary. Next to early retirees, one could also look at the chances of reentry of unemployed older workers. With the increasing unemployment rates among workers 50+ (Statistics Netherland, 2012), they form a significant share of potential applicants. Moreover, there are also workers who are currently employed or self-employed but are considering changing their job. Workers' employment history might signal older workers qualities (Thurow, 1972) and prolonged exit from the labour force is associated with decreasing human capital. Comparison of different categories of older works might offer a fruitful avenue towards disentangling the dynamics of hiring at older ages.

Also, in the analysis of the hiring of older workers one might want to look at the different types of contract that older workers are offered. I looked at hiring of older early retirees and differentiated worker preferences for full-time employment as opposed to part-time. Although this approach offered the possibility to model different employment choices of managers in terms of the time frame for which they intend to hire early retirees, more insight into the content of the contracts might shed light on employment desirability. There is evidence that suggests that older workers are often valued for their specific knowledge or skills and are often hired as consultants, advisor or freelancers (Platman and Tinker, 1998). With the current design I was not able to determine if this selective hiring does take place. More research on this topic is thus necessary.

This dissertation also attempted to disentangle what factors affected managers offering training opportunities for individual older workers and showed, next to the importance of workers' own personal circumstances, that managers' decisions were not dependent on the types of training or the cost involved. There are two possible explanations for these findings. On the one hand, one might assume that there is indeed no difference in how managers evaluate different types of training. Another possibility is that the design of the study was not sufficient to disentangle those differences. One cannot rule out the possibility that the distinction between costs and goals of training did not reflect the reality of respondents' specific organisational settings and therefore, managers had difficulties evaluating the desirability of those types of training. Given the importance of training for older workers, an additional attempt with differently specified time and cost schemes is necessary to gain more insight into the differences in training the training opportunities.

Moreover, in this study I did not evaluate whether the content of training makes a difference to managers. One might argue that what workers learn can be of variable use for organisations and consequently it might affect managers' idea of the necessity for such training. Future research should evaluate whether training opportunities are dependent on the content of the training.

6.4. Methodological considerations

The current study applied a two-stage design. The process of data collection was facilitated by the LISS Internet panel survey which holds monthly survey interviews with a representative sample of the Dutch population. Cooperation with the LISS panel granted not only access to managers participating in the panel but also the possibility to approach those respondents twice, after a short period of time. Managers were first presented with questions on attitudes towards older workers, and a month later the same respondents were approached again to participate in vignette experiments.

This approach was successful for three reasons. Firstly, it offered access to the sample of managers, a group of respondents who are traditionally considered difficult to reach for experimental designs (Remus, 1986). Consequently, I assume that the external validity of the results presented in this study increased. Secondly, an application of vignettes enabled modeling a (hypothetical) decision making process. As pointed out by Oosterhuis and Glebbeek (1990), vignettes offer a better representation of employment procedures than is the case with a traditional survey. Natural experiments might offer a still better opportunity to assess managers' hiring decisions that managers take with respect to older workers, yet gathering data on real-life hiring decisions is difficult.

Thirdly, through the implementation of both parts of the study separately (with a monthly gap between the two studies), this data offer a possibility to model the impact of general attitudes on employment decisions regarding specific older workers. Despite the clear advantages of this approach and the multistage design, I cannot rule out the risk of social desirability bias that might have occurred when managers were primed with the survey and later asked to participate in the vignette experiment (Pager and Quillian, 2005). Nonetheless, I propose that the limited exposure of respondents to the questions about older workers and the time span that passed between two studies lowers the risk of carry over effects and related bias.

Despite those advantages, this method has some disadvantages. There is evidence that vignette studies may lead to underestimation of the discriminatory attitudes in employment decisions as compared to field studies (Pager and Quillian, 2005). Also, one has to keep in mind that managers assessed hypothetical situations. In real life, hiring participants may act or decide differently. This dissertation nonetheless showed that the validity of the results obtained with of the vignette study was confirmed; the results of a replication study on hiring of early retirees on a bigger sample of managers were consistent with the results obtained from a pilot study.

The LISS Internet panel has proven to be an excellent tool for gathering valuable data for the purpose of this dissertation. Those kinds of surveys are not accessible everywhere though. Consequently, researchers who study employment decisions might face limited opportunity to implement a multistage design and restricted access to manager samples. The first empirical chapter of this dissertation points towards an alternative in approaching respondents. For this chapter the data was collected during a focus group meeting organized at NIDI and participating managers were asked to fill in the vignette experiments. Managers frequently participate in focus groups meetings (Brines and De Vos, 2001; Truss, 20001; Hope *et al.*, 2005) and collecting the data during such a meeting is an established procedure (Beaulieu *et al.*, 1999). Conducting of vignette experiments during focus groups meetings might constitute a good alternative to applying student samples that were often criticised for the lack of experience with the decisions they were evaluating (Remus, 1999). The quality of the data obtained for this dissertation during a focus group meeting was satisfactory, and the results of this study were later corroborated with the data collected through access to the LISS panel survey.

6.5. Concluding remarks

The current study focused on the decisions that managers take with respect to the hiring of early retirees, older workers' retention and training opportunities and evaluated how individual, organisational and managers' characteristics contribute to these decisions. The results presented in four empirical chapters indicate that managers are involved in complex considerations that are affected by various factors.

All the studies have manifested the importance of older workers' employability. At the same time, the context of organisations is also critical for the possibility to hire, retain or train those workers. Although individual characteristics of older workers and organisational forces contribute importantly towards their chances for hiring, being offered training opportunities and retention, employers are key players in defining the opportunities for retirement and opportunities for working longer (Shultz and Henkens, 2010). As managers are not very positive towards extending employment of older workers, they may form barriers towards their employment.

This conclusion leads to few practical recommendations to increase the labour market participation of older workers. On the one hand, investment in the employability of older workers appears to be crucial. Workers, who miss relevant experience, are not flexible or in frail health stand few chances to extend their working career. Therefore investments in life-long learning or policies that promote a healthy life style are among the tools that can prepare future older workers to the challenges of an extended working life.

On the other hand, polices aimed at imposing restrictions might also contribute to increase labour market participation of older workers. One of the attempts to stimulate such participation were changes in the Dutch pension system, which restricted exit opportunities. According to the new policies, access to early retirement schemes has been restricted, and at the same time the age eligibility for state pension age has been raised from 65 to 67. Also, the application of alternative exit schemes (*e.g.* disability schemes) has been restricted. Once exit paths are closed, organisations need to implement more proactive policies to maintain productive employment of their older staff than only implementing ergonomical measures (Conen *et al.*, 2011).

The attitudes of managers towards older workers definitely cannot be omitted. This study shows that older workers will not be welcome in the labour-force without managers' support. These findings stress the need for awareness campaigns that will demonstrate the impact of age norms in the employment process. Research has shown that executives agree that older workers are discriminated against, but do not believe that this occures in their own organisations (Maurer *et al.*, 2007). Secondly, training of recruiters towards more age awareness in selection procedures is necessary and in the long run can benefit both organisations and older workers by selecting better candidates and creating diversity in teams. Preventing the potential bias of age norms has also implications for older workers who are employed in organisations. As managers have a rather clear idea as to when a person should leave the labour force, such attitudes can result in reduced access of older workers to training or lack of managerial support for employment until the statutory retirement age.

An ageing of the population is a growing concern of many governments, and an increased labour market participation of older workers is one measure to deal with challenges brought about by demographic changes which threaten the stability of social security systems (OECD, 2006). The number of older workers who remain active in paid labour depends strongly on the policies implemented in organisations. Despite widespread discussion in the media and society, older workers leave even earlier than at age 65. This dissertation showed that when promoting prolonged and effective employment of older workers it is important to take into account not only workers and their qualifications and abilities but also to actively promote organisational structures and implement polices to reduce managers' prejudices.

References

Acemoglu, D. and J.-S. Pischke (1999), The structure of wages and investment in general training. *Journal of Political Economy*, 107, pp. 539-572.

Aguinis, H. and K. Kraiger (2009), Benefits of training and development for individuals and teams, organisations, and society. *Annual Review of Psychology*, 60, pp. 451-474.

Armstrong-Stassen, M. and A. Templer (2005), Adapting training for older employees: The Canadian response to an aging workforce. *Journal of Management Development*, 24(1), pp. 57-67.

Armstrong-Stassen, M. and J. Cattaneo (2010), The effect of downsizing on organisational practices targeting older workers. *Journal of Management Development*, 29(4), pp. 344-363.

Avolio, B.J. and V.G. Barret (1987), Effect of age stereotyping in a simulated interview. *Psychology and Aging*, 2(1), pp. 56-63.

Balkin, D.B. and N. Richebé (2007), A gift exchange perspective on organisational training. *Human Resource Management Review*, 17(1), pp. 52-62.

Bargh, J.A., M. Chen and L. Burrows (1996), Automaticity of social behavior: Direct effects of trait construct and stereotype activation on action. *Journal of Personality and Social Psychology*, 71(2), pp. 230-244.

Barr, S.H. and M.A. Hitt (1986), A comparison of selection decision-models in manager versus student samples. *Personnel Psychology*, 39(3), pp. 599-617.

Barrett, A. and P.J. O'Connell (2001), Does training generally work? The returns to in-company training. *Industrial and Labor Relations Review*, 54(3), pp. 647-662.

Bassanini, A., A. Booth, G. Brunello, M. de Paola and E. Leuven (2005), Workplace training in Europe. IZA Discussion Paper (no. 1640), Bonn.

Beaulieu, M.-D., E. Hudon, D. Roberge, R. Pineault, D. Forté and J. Légaré (1999), Practice guidelines for clinical prevention: Do patients, physicians and experts share common ground? *Canadian Medical Association*, 161(5), pp. 519-523.

Becker, G.S. (1957), The economics of discrimination. Chicago: University of Chicago Press.

Becker, G.S. (1975), Human capital, a theoretical and empirical analysis with special reference to education., 2nd ed. New York: Columbia U.P.

Beehr, T.A., D.M. Weisbrodt and M.J. Zagumny (1994), Satisfaction with subordinates: A neglected research issue concerning supervisors. *Journal of Applied Social Psychology*, 24(18), pp. 1665-1684.

Beek, K. van, C. Koopmans and B. van Praag (1997), Shopping at the labour market: A real tale of fiction. *European Economic Review*, 41(2), pp. 295-317.

Bendick, M., C.W. Jackson and J.H. Romero (1997), Employment discrimination against older workers — an experimental study of hiring practices. *Journal of Ageing and Social Policy*, 8(4), pp. 25-46.

Berger, E.D. (2009), Managing age discrimination: An examination of the techniques used when seeking employment. *The Gerontologist*, 49(3), pp. 317-332.

Bishop, J. (1997), What we know about employer-provided training: A review of the literature. *Research in Labor Economics*, 16, pp. 19-87.

Blanchard, O.J. and L.H. Summers (1986), Hysteresis and the European unemployment problem. In S. Fischer (ed.), *NBER Macroeconomics Annual*. Cambridge, Massachusetts: MIT Press, pp. 15-78.

Borghans, L., D. Fouarge and A. de Grip (2011), *Een leven lang leren in Nederland*. No. ROA-R-2011/5). Maastricht: Researchcentrum voor Onderwijs en Arbeidsmarkt (ROA). Maastricht University: School of Business and Economics.

Boudon, R. (1987), The individualistic tradition in sociology. In J.C. Alexander, B. Giesen, R. Munch and N.J. Smelser (eds.), *The micro-macro link* (pp. 45-70). Berkeley California: University of California Press.

Brown, K.G. and T. Sitzmann (2011), Training and employee development for improved performance. In S. Zedeck (ed.), *APA handbook of industrial and organisational psychology*, vol 2: Selecting and developing members for the organisation. APA handbooks in psychology (pp. 469-503). Washington, DC, US: American Psychological Association.

Bruce, D., D. Holtz-Eakin and J. Quinn (2000), Self-employment and labor market transitions at older ages. Center for Retirement Research at Boston College Working Paper 2000-13, Available online at http://escholarship.bc.edu/retirement papers/33 [Accessed 29 March 2010].

CPB (2000), *Ageing in the Netherlands*. The Hague: Centraal Planbureau. Government of the Netherlands, 2012.

CEC (Commission of the European Communities) (2000), A memorandum on lifelong learning. Brussels, Belgium: European Commission.

Chiu, W.C., A.W. Chan, E. Snape and T. Redman (2001), Age stereotypes and discriminatory attitudes towards older workers: An East-West comparison. *Human Relations*, 54(5), pp. 629-661.

Conen, W. (2012), Older workers: The view of Dutch employers in a European perspective. Disseration: Utrecht University: Utrecht School of Economics.

Conen, W., K. Henkens and J.J. Schippers (2011), Are employers changing their behavior toward older workers? An analysis of employers' surveys 2000-2009. *Journal of Aging & Social Policy*, 23(2), pp. 141-158.

Conen, W.S., K. Henkens and J.J. Schippers (2012), Employers' attitudes and actions towards the extension of working lives in Europe. *International Journal of Manpower*, 33(6), pp. 648-665.

Coleman, J. (1990), Foundations of social theory. Cambridge, Massachusetts: The Belknap Press of Harvard University Press.

Cropanzano, R. and M.S. Mitchell (2005), Social exchange theory: An interdisciplinary review. *Journal of Management*, 31(6), pp. 874-900.

Cully, M., A. vandenHeuvel, M. Wooden and R. Curtain (2001), Barriers to training of older workers and possible policy solutions. Analysis and Equity Branch, Commonwealth; Department of Education, Training and Youth Affairs.

Dalen, H.P. van and K. Henkens (2002), Early-retirement reform: Can it and will it work? *Ageing and Society*, 22(2), pp. 209-232.

Dalen, H.P. van, K. Henkens, B. Lokhorst and J.J. Schippers (2009), Herintreding van vroeggepensioneerden. Onderzoeksrapport 9-9-2009. Den Haag: Raad voor Werk en Inkomen.

Dalen, H.P. van, K. Henkens and J.J. Schippers (2010a), How do employers cope with an ageing workforce? Views from employers and employees. *Demographic Research*, 22, pp. 1015-1036.

Dalen, H.P. van, K. Henkens and J.J. Schippers (2010b), Productivity of older workers: perceptions of employers and employees. *Population and Development Review*, 36(2), pp. 309-330.

Damman, M., K. Henkens and M. Kalmijn (2013), Late-career work disengagement: the role of proximity to retirement and career experiences. *Journals of Gerontology, Series B: Psychological Sciences and Social Sciences*.

Daniel, K. and J.S. Heywood (2007), The determinants of hiring older workers: UK evidence. *Labour Economics*, 14(1), pp. 35-51.

Das, T.K. (2003), Managerial perceptions and the essence of the managerial world: What is an interloper business executive to make of the academic-researcher perceptions of managers? *British Journal of Management*, 14(1), pp. 23-32.

Davies, R. and P. Elias (2004), Employer provided training within the European union: A comparative review. In C. Sofer (ed.), *Human capital over the life cycle. A European perspective.* Edward Elgar publishing, Northampton Massachusets, pp. 137-153.

Dedrick, E. and G.H. Dobbins (1991), The influence of subordinate age on managerial actions: An attributional analysis. *Journal of Organisational Behavior*, 12(5), pp. 367-377.

DiNatale, M. (2001), Characteristics of and preference for alternative work arrangements, 1999. *Monthly Labor Review*, 124(3), pp. 28-49.

Dohmen, D. and D. Timmermann (2010), *Financing adult learning in time of crisis.* Brussels: EU Knowledge System for Lifelong Learning.

Doorne-Huiskes, A. van and J.J. Schippers (2010), Vrouwen op de arbeidsmarkt: een succesvolle worsteling. *Tijdschrift voor Arbeidsvraagstukken*, 4, pp. 400-416.

Duncan, C. and W. Loretto (2004), Never the right age? Gender and age-based discrimination in employment. *Gender, Work and Organisation*, 11(1), pp. 95-115.

Eijs, P. van and H. Heijke (2000), Mismatch between occupation and education and the costs and benefits of job related training. In H. Heijke and J. Muysken (eds.), *Education and training in a knowledge-based economy.* Macmillan, London, pp. 159-189.

Ekerdt, D.J. (2010), Frontiers of research on work and retirement. *Journals of Gerontology*, Series B-Psychological Sciences and Social Sciences, 65(1), pp. 69-80.

Elster, J. (1989), Social norms and economic-theory. *Journal of Economic Perspectives*, 3(4), pp. 99-117.

Etzioni, A. (2000), Social norms: Internalization, persuasion, and history. *Law & Society Review*, 34(1), pp. 157-178.

Eurobarometer (2012), *Active ageing. Special eurobarometer*. No. 378. Brussels: Directorate-General for Employment, Social Affairs and Inclusion.

European Commission (2006), Employment in Europe 2006. Brussels: European Commission.

European Commission (2010), The European social fund and older workers. Brussels: European Commission.

Eurostat's Demography Database (2012).

Euwals, R., R. de Mooij and D. van Vuuren (2009), *Rethinking retirement*. Netherlands Bureau for Economic Policy Analysis [CBP] No 80. The Hague: CBP.

Eyster, L., R.W. Johnson and E. Toder (2008), *Current strategies to employ and recruit older workers*. Washington, DC: The Urban Institute. http://www.urban.org/url.cfm?ID=411626. [Accessed 23 April 2011].

Fazzio, R. (1990), How do attitudes guide bahavior? In E.T. Higgins and R.M. Sorrentino (eds.), *Handbook of motivation and cognition*, Volume 2: Foundations of Social Behavior. New York, N.Y.: The Guilford Press, pp. 204-244.

Finkelstein, L.M. and M.J. Burke (1998), Age stereotyping at work: The role of rater and contextual factors on evaluation of job applicants. *Journal of General Psychology*, 125, pp. 317-345.

Finkelstein, L.M., M.J. Burke and N.S. Raju (1995), Age discrimination in simulated employment contexts: An integrative analysis. *Journal of Applied Psychology*, 80(6), pp. 652-663.

Fouarge, D., T. Schils and A. de Grip (2010), Why do low-educated workers invest less in further training? ROA, Research Memoranda 2010/10. Maastricht: Research Centre for Education and the Labour Market.

Fugate, M., A.J. Kinicki and B.E. Ashforth (2004), Employability: A psycho-social construct, its dimensions, and applications. *Journal of Vocational Behavior*, 65(1), pp. 14-38.

Ganong, L.H. and M. Coleman (2006), Multiple segment factorial vignette designs. *Journal of Marriage and Family*, 68(2), pp. 455-468.

Gellatly, I.R. (1995), Individual and group determinants of employee absenteeism: A test of a causal model. *Journal of Organisational Behavior*, 16(5), pp. 469-85.

Gordon, M.E., L.A. Slade and N. Schmitt (1987), Student guinea pigs: Porcine predictors and particularistic phenomena. *The Academy of Management Review*, 12(1), pp. 160-163.

Gould, W. (2002), Chow test. STATA Website. Available online at http://www.stata. com/support/faqs/stat/chow3.html. [Accessed 27 October 2009].

Government of the Netherlands (2012), AOW-leeftijd stapsgewijs omhoog naar 66 jaar in 2019 en 67 jaar in 2023. Persbericht 25-05-2012.

Hailey, V.H., E. Farndale and C. Truss (2005), The HR department's role in organisational performance. *Human Resource Management Journal*, 15(3), pp. 49-66.

Hardy, M.A. (2002), The transformation of retirement in twentieth- century America: From discontent to satisfaction. *Generations*, 26(2), pp. 9-16.

Hassell, B. and P.L. Perrewe (1995), An examination of beliefs about older workers: Do stereotypes still exist? *Journal of Organisational Behaviour*, 16(5), pp. 457-68.

Hayward, M.D. and M.A. Hardy (1985), Early retirement processes among older men. *Research on Aging*, 7(4), pp. 491-515.

Henkens, K. (1999), Retirement intentions and spousal support: A multiactor approach. *Journal of Gerontology*, Social Sciences, 54B, pp. 63-74.

Henkens, K. (2005), Stereotyping older workers and retirement: The managers' point of view. *Canadian Journal on Aging*, 24(4), pp. 353-366.

Henkens, K. and H. van Dalen (2013),The employer's perspective on retirement. In M. Wang (ed.) *The Oxford Handbook of Retirement* (pp. 215-227). New York: Oxford University Press.

Henkens, K., H.P. van Dalen and H. van Solinge (2009), *De vervagende grens tussen werk en pensioen; over doorwerkers, doorstarters en herintreders* [The blurring borders between work and retirement]. NIDI Report 78. Amsterdam: KNAW Press.

Henkens, K., H. van Solinge and R. Cozijnsen (2009), Let go or retain? A comparative study of the attitudes of business students and managers about the retirement of older workers. *Journal of Applied Social Psychology*, 39(7), pp. 1562-1588.

Henkens, K., H. van Solinge and H. van Dalen (2013), *Doorwerken over de drempel van pensioen*. NIDI Book 87. Amsterdam: Amsterdam University Press.

Hilton, J.L. and W. von Hippel (1996), Stereotypes. *Annual Review of Psychology*, 47, pp. 237-271.

Horne, C. (2003), The internal enforcement of norms. *European Sociological Review*, 19(4), pp. 335-343.

Hox, J.J. (2002), Multilevel analysis: Techniques and applications. New Jersey: Erlbaum, Mahwah.

Jacobs, M.A., A. van Doorne-Huiskes, J.J. Schippers and J.J. Siegers (1990), Werving en selectie van vrouwen bij de politie. *Tijdschrift voor arbeidsvraagstukken*, 6, pp. 22-38.

Johnson, R.W. (2009), Employment opportunities at older ages. Introduction to the Special Issue. *Research on Aging*, 31(1), pp. 3-16.

Jones, D.A. and B.R. McIntosh (2010), Organisational and occupational commitment in relation to bridge employment and retirement intentions. *Journal of Vocational Behavior*, 77(2), pp. 290-303.

Jorgensen, B. and P. Taylor (2008), Older workers, government and business: Implications for ageing populations of a globalizing economy. *Economic Affairs*, 28(1), pp. 17-22.

Karpinska, K., K. Henkens and J.J. Schippers (2011), The recruitment of early retirees: A vignette study of the factors that affect managers' decisions. *Ageing & Society*, 31(4), pp. 570-589.

Karpinska, K., K. Henkens and J.J. Schippers (2013), Hiring retirees: Impact of age norms and stereotypes. *Journal of Managerial Psychology*. (Forthcoming)

Kalleberg, A.L., D. Knoke, P.V. Marsden and J.L. Spaeth (1996), Organisations in America: Analyzing their structures and human resource practices. California: Sage, Thousand Oaks.

Kim, S. and D.C. Feldman (2000), Working in retirement: The antecedents of bridge employment and its consequences for quality of life in retirement. *Academy of Management Journal*, 43(6), pp. 1195-1210.

Kapteyn, A. and K. de Vos (1998), Social security and labor-force participation in the Netherlands. *The American Economic Review*, 88(2), pp. 164-167.

Koppes, L.L.J., E.M.M. de Vroome, M.E.M. Mol, B.J.M. Janssen and S.N.J. van den Bossche (2009), Nationale Enquête Arbeidsomstandigheden 2008 [National Labour Force Survey 2008]. Delft, the Netherlands: Nederlandse Organisatie voor Toegepast Natuurwetenschappelijk Onderzoek (TNO).

Lawrence, B.S. (1996), Organisational age norms: Why is it so hard to know one when you see one? *Gerontologist*, 36(2), pp. 209-220.

Lazazzara, A., K. Karpinska and K. Henkens (2013), What factors influence training opportunities for older workers? Three factorial surveys exploring the attitudes of HR professionals. *The International Journal of Human Resource Management*. (Forthcoming)

Lee, J. and C. Clemons (1985), Factors affecting employment decisions about older workers. *Journal of Applied Psychology*, 70(4), pp. 785-788.

Leeuw, E.D., J. Hox and D.A. Dillman (2008), International handbook of survey methodology. New York: Lawrence Erlbaum Associates.

Leuven, E. and H. Oosterbeek (1999), Demand and supply of work-related training: Evidence from four countries. *Research in Labor Economics*, 18, pp. 303-30.

Leuven, E. and H. Oosterbeek (2004), Evaluating the effect of tax deductions on training. *Journal of Labor Economics*, 22(1), pp. 461-488.

Liefbroer, A.C. (2009), European opinions on the timing of retirement. European Policy Brief. Available at: http://www.multilinks-project.eu/uploads/papers/0000/0024/Second_Policy_Brief_MULTILINKS.pdf [accessed 12 December 2011].

Liefbroer, A.C. and F.C. Billari (2010), Bringing norms back in: A theoretical and empirical discussion of their importance for understanding demographic behaviour. *Population, Space and Place*, 16(4), pp. 287-305.

Loretto, W., C. Duncan and P. White (2000), Ageism and employment: controversies, ambiguities and younger people's perceptions. *Ageing & Society*, 20(3), pp. 279-302.

Loretto, W. and P. White (2006), Employers' attitudes, practices and policies towards older workers. *Human Resource Management Journal*, 16(3), pp. 313-330.

Macrae, C.N. and G.V. Bodenhausen (2001), Social cognition: Categorical person Perception. *British Journal of Psychology*, 92, pp. 239-255.

Marini, M. (1992), The role of models of purposive action in sociology. In J.S. Coleman and T.J. Farraro (eds.), *Rational choice theory. Advocacy and critique.* London: Sage, pp. 21-48.

Marsden, P.V. and E. Garman (2001), Social networks, job search and recruitment. In I.E. Berg and A.L. Kalleberg (eds.), *Sourcebook of labor markets: Evolving structures and processes.* New York: Kluwer Academic/Plenum Publisher, pp. 476-502.

Martin, J. and J.W. Harder (1994), Bread and roses: Justice and the distribution of financial and socioemotional rewards in organisations. *Social Justice Research*, 7, pp. 241-264.

Mathieu, J.E. and D.M. Zajac (1990), A review and meta-analysis of the antecedents, correlates and consequences of organisational commitment. *Psychological Bulletin*, 108, pp. 171-194.

Maurer, T., F. Barbeite, E. Weiss and M. Lippstreu (2007), New measures of stereotypical beliefs about older workers' ability and desire for development. Exploration among employees aged 40 and over. *Journal of Managerial Psychology*, 23(4), pp. 395-418.

McCann, R. and H. Giles (2002), Ageism and the workplace: A communication perspective. In T.D. Nelson (ed.), *Ageism, stereotyping and prejudice against older person.* Cambridge, Massachusetts: MIT Press, pp. 163-199.

McGregor, J. and L. Gray (2002), Stereotyping older workers: New Zealand experience. *Social Policy Journal of New Zealand*, 18, pp. 163-177.

McNair, S., M. Flynn and Y. Dutton (2007), Employer responses to an ageing workforce: A qualitative study. London: Department for Work and Pensions. Available from http://research.dwp.gov.uk/asd/asd5/rports2007-2008/rrep455.pdf [Accessed 23 March 2010].

Michellone, G. and G. Zollo (2000), Competencies management in knowledge-based firms. *International Journal of Technology Management*, 20(1-2), pp. 134-155.

Ministery of Social Affairs and Employment (2011), Brief van minister Kamp over het Vitaliteitspakket, available online http://www.rijksoverheid.nl/documenten-en-publicaties/kamerstukken/2011/07/04/brief-van-minister-kamp-over-het-vitaliteitspakket.html [Accessed September 16 2012].

Molm, L.D. (1994), Dependence and risk — transforming and structure of social-exchange. *Social Psychology Quarterly*, 57(3), pp. 163-176.

Munnell, A.H. and S.A. Sass (2008), Working longer. The solution to the retirement income challenge. Washington: The Brookings Institutions.

Munnell, A.H., S.A. Sass and M. Soto (2006), Employers attitudes towards older workers: Survey results. An Issue in Brief Center for the Retirement Research, Boston College (series 3).

Ng, T.W.H. and D.C. Feldman (2008), The relationship of age to ten dimensions of job performance. *Journal of Applied Psychology*, 93(2), pp. 392-423.

Nimwegen, N. van, G.C.N. Beets, J.J. Schoorl and P. Ekamper (2011), *Demography report 2010: Older, more numerous and diverse Europeans.* [Collab.]. Brussels: European Commission.

Organisation for Economic Co-operation and Development (OECD) (2003), *Beyond rhetoric. Adult learning policies and practices.* Paris France: OECD.

Organisation for Economic Co-operation and Development (OECD) (2006), *Live Longer, Work Longer.* Paris France: OECD.

Pager. D. and L. Quillian (2005), Walking the talk? What employers say versus what they do. *American Sociological Review*, 70(3), pp. 355-380.

Perry, E., C. Kulik and A. Bourhis (1996), Moderating effects of personal and contextual factors in age discrimination. *Journal of Applied Psychology*, 81(6), pp. 628-647.

Peterson, R. (2001), On the use of college students in social science research: Insights from a second order meta analysis. *Journal of Consumer Research*, 28(3), pp. 450-461.

Phelps, E.S. (1972), The statistical theory of racism and sexism. *American Economic Review*, 62(4), pp. 659-661.

Platman, K. and A. Tinker (1998), Getting on in the BBC: A case study of older workers. *Aging and Society*, 18(5), pp. 513-535.

Posthuma, R.A. and M.A. Campion (2009), Age stereotypes in the workplace: Common stereotypes, Moderators and future research directions. *Journal of Management*, 35(1), pp. 158-188.

Rainbird, H. (2000), Skilling the unskilled: Access to work-based learning and the lifelong learning agenda. *Journal of Education and Work*, 13(2), pp. 183-197.

Remery, C., K. Henkens, J.J. Schippers and P. Ekamper (2003), Managing an aging workforce and a tight labor market: Views held by Dutch employers. *Population Research and Policy Review*, 22(1), pp. 21-40.

Remus, W. (1996), Will behavioral research on managerial decision making generalize to managers? *Managerial and Decision Economics*, 17(1), pp. 93-101.

Government of the Netherlands (2012), *Mobiliteitsbonus voor werkgevers.* Regeerakkoord 2012.

Robbins, S.P. (1993), Organisational behaviour. concepts, controversies and applications (6th ed.). Englewood Cliffs, NJ: Prentice-Hall.

Roscigno, V.J., S. Mong, R. Byron and G. Tester (2007), Age discrimination, social closure and employment. *Social Forces*, 86, pp. 313-334.

Rosen, B., T.H. Jerdee and R.O. Lunn (1981), Effects of performance appraisal format, age, and performance level on retirement decisions. *Journal of Applied Psychology*, 66(4), pp. 515-519.

Rossi, P.H. and A.B. Anderson (1982), Measuring social judgments. The factorial survey approach: An introduction. In P.H. Rossi and S.L. Nock (eds.), *Measuring social judgments: The factorial survey approach*. California, Beverley Hills: Sage, pp. 15-67.

Salganik, M.J. and D.D. Heckathorn (2004), Sampling and estimation in hidden populations using respondent-driven sampling. *Sociological Methodology*, 34(1), pp. 193-239.

Sears, D.O. (1996), College sophomores in the laboratory: Influences of a narrow data base on social psychology's view of human nature. *Journal of Personality and Social Psychology*, 51(3), pp. 515-530.

Settersten, R.A. and G.O. Hagestad (1996), What's the latest? II. Cultural age deadlines for educational and work transitions. *The Gerontologist*, 36(5), pp. 602-613.

Settersten, R.A. (1998), Time, age, and the transition to retirement: New evidence on life-course flexibility? *International Journal of Aging & Human Development*, 47(3), pp. 177-203.

Shore, L.M., J.N. Cleveland and C.B. Goldberg (2003), Work attitudes and decisions as a function of manager age and employee age. *Journal of Applied Psychology*, 88(3), pp. 529-537.

Shultz, K.S. and C.J.I.M. Henkens (2010), Introduction to the changing nature of retirement: An international perspective [Guest editorial]. *International Journal of Manpower*, 31(3), pp. 265-270.

Singer, M.S. and C. Sewell (1989), Applicant age and selection interview decisions: Effect of information exposure on age discrimination in personnel selection *Personnel Psychology*, 42(1), pp. 135-154.

Smeaton, D., S. Vegeris and M. Sahin-Dikmen (2010), Older workers: Employment preferences, barriers and solutions. Research Report 43. Manchester: Equality and Human Rights Commission Research Report Series. Available online at http://www. equalityhumanrights.com/uploaded_files/research/older_workers_employment_ preferences_barriers_and_solutions_v2.pdf [Accessed 23 March 2010].

Solinge, H. van and K. Henkens (2007), Involuntary retirement: The role of restrictive circumstances, timing, and social embeddedness. *Journal of Gerontology*, 62B(5), pp. 295-303.

Spence, M. (1973), Job market signalling. *Quarterly Journal of Economics*, 87(3), pp. 355-374.

Stata (2003), Stata reference manual. Volume 3, N-R Release 8. Texas: Stata Press, College Station.

Statistics Netherlands (2012a), *Levensverwachting: geslacht en leeftijd, vanaf 1950*. Statline.

Statistics Netherlands (2012b), *Bevolking; geslacht, leeftijd en burgerlijke staat, 1 januari (1950-2010)*. Statline.

Statistics Netherlands (2012c), *Bevolking; leeftijd, geslacht, herkomstgroepering en generatie 2011-2060*. Statline.

Statistics Netherlands (2012d), *Van arbeid naar pensioen; personen 55 jaar of ouder*. Statline.

Statistics Netherlands (2012e), *Beroepsbevolking; geslacht en leeftijd*. Statline.

Statistics Netherlands (2012f), *Post-initieel onderwijs, levenslang leren: deelname naar enkele kenmerken*. Statline.

Steedman, H. and S. McIntosh (2001), *Measuring low skills in europe: How useful is the ISCED framework?* Oxford Economic Papers-New Series, 53(3), pp. 564-581.

Sterns, H.L. and J. Kaplan (2003), Self-management of career and retirement. In G.A. Adams and T.A. Beehr (eds.), Retirement, reasons, processes and results. New York: Springer Publishing Company, pp. 188-214.

Stichting van de Arbeid (2011), *Uitwerkingsmemorandum pensioenakkoord 2010 en Beleidsagenda 2020*. Den Haag: SVDA.

Taylor, P. (2008). Are European older workers on the verge of a 'golden age' of employment opportunities? In A. Chiva and J. Manthorpe (eds.), *Older Workers in Europe*. UK, Maidenhead: Open University Press, pp. 38-52.

Taylor, P. and A. Walker (1994), The aging workforce: Employers' attitudes towards older people. *Work, Employment and Society*, 8(4), pp. 569-591.

Taylor, P. and A. Walker (1998a), Employers and older workers: Attitudes and employment practices. *Ageing & Society*, 18(6), pp. 641-658.

Taylor, P. and A. Walker (1998b), Policies and practices towards older workers: A framework for comparative research. *Human Resource Management Journal*, 8(3), pp. 61-76.

Taylor, P. (2008), Are European older workers on the verge of a 'golden age' of employment opportunities? In A. Chiva and J. Manthorpe (eds.), *Older workers in Europe*. UK, Maidenhead: Open University Press, pp. 38-52.

Tazelaar, F. (1982), From a oassical attitude behavior-hypothesis to a general model of behavior via the theory of mental incongruity. In W. Raub (ed.), *Theoretical models and empirical analyses. Contributions to the explanation of individual actions and collective phenomena*. Utrecht, the Netherlands: E.S. Publications, pp. 101-128.

Thurow, L.C. (1975), *Generating inequality: Mechanisms of distribution in the US*. New York: Basic Books.

Torraco, R.J. (2000), A theory of knowledge management. *Advances in Developing Human Resources*, 2(1), pp. 38-62.

Truss, C. (2001), Complexities and controversies in linking HRM with organisational outcomes. *Journal of Management Studies*, 38(8), pp. 1121-1149.

UWV (2012), *Vacatures in Nederland 2011. De vacaturemarkt en personeelswerving in beeld*.

Vickerstaff, S., W. Loretto, J. Billings, P. Brown, L. Mitton, T. Parkin and P. White (2008), Encouraging labour market activity among 60-64 year olds. Research Report 531. London: Department for Work and Pensions. Available from: http://www.dwp.gov.uk/asd/asd5/rrs-index.asp [Accessed 29 March 2010].

Von Bonsdorff, M.E., K.S. Shultz, E. Leskinen and J. Tansky (2009), The choice between retirement and bridge employment: A continuity theory and life course perspective. *International Journal of Aging & Human Development*, 69(2), pp. 79-100.

Wallander, L. (2009), 25 years of factorial surveys in sociology: A review. *Social Science Research*, 38(3), pp. 505-520.

Wang, M. and K.S. Shultz (2010), Employee retirement: A review and recommendations for future investigation. *Journal of Management*, 36(1), pp. 172-206.

Wang, M., Y. Zhan, S. Liu and K.S. Shultz (2008), Antecedents of bridge employment: A longitudinal investigation. *Journal of Applied Psychology*, 93(4), pp. 818-830.

Warr, P. and J. Pennington (1993), Views about age discrimination and older workers. In P.A. Taylor, A. Walker, B. Casey, H. Metcalf, J. Lakey, P. Warr and J. Pennington (eds.), *Age and employment: Policies, attitudes and practice*. London: Institute of Personnel Management, pp. 75-106.

Weckerle, J.R. and K.S. Shultz (1999), Influences on the bridge employment decision among older USA workers. *Journal of Occupational and Organisational Psychology*, 72, pp. 317-329.

Wolf, I. de and R. van der Velden (2001), Selection processes for three types of academic jobs. An experiment among Dutch employers of social sciences graduates. *European Sociological Review*, 17(3), pp. 317-330.

List of NIDI books/reports

89. Kasia Karpinska, *Prolonged employment of older workers. Determinants of managers' decisions regarding hiring, retention and training*, 2013, pp. 143.
88. Wieteke Conen, *Older workers: The view of Dutch employers in a European perspective*, 2013, pp. 162.
87. Kène Henkens, Harry van Dalen en Hanna van Solinge, *Doorwerken over de drempel van het pensioen (Working beyond retirement)*, 2013, pp. 124.
86. Nico van Nimwegen en Carlo van Praag (red.), *Bevolkingsvraagstukken in Nederland anno 2012: actief ouder worden in Nederland (Population issues in the Netherlands, 2012: active ageing in the Netherlands)*, Werkverband Periodieke Rapportage Bevolkingsvraagstukken, 2012, pp. 195.
85. Harry van Dalen, Kène Henkens, Wieteke Conen en Joop Schippers, *Dilemma's rond langer doorwerken: Europese werkgevers aan het woord. (Dilemmas in active ageing: What do European employers say)*, 2012, pp. 128.
84. Marcel Ham en Jelle van der Meer, *De etnische bril: Categorisering in het integratiebeleid*, 2012, pp. 72.
83. Joop de Beer, *Transparency in population forecasting: Methods for fitting and projecting fertility, mortality and migration.* 2011, pp. 256.
82. Nico van Nimwegen, *Demography Monitor 2008. Demographic trends, socio-economic impacts and policy implications in the European Union*, 2010, pp. 161.
81. Judith P.M. Soons, *Love, life and happiness: A study of partner relationships and well-being in young adulthood*, 2009, pp. 175.
80. Nico van Nimwegen en Liesbeth Heering, *Bevolkingsvraagstukken in Nederland anno 2009: Van groei naar krinp. Een demografische omslag in beeld. (Population issues in the Netherlands, 2009: From population growth to decline. Perspectives on a demographic turning point)*, 2009, pp. 240.
79. Anne Elisabeth van Putten, *The role of intergenerational transfers in gendered labour patterns*, 2009, pp. 215.
78. Kène Henkens, Harry van Dalen en Hanna van Solinge, *De vervagende grens tussen werk en pensioen: over doorwerkers, doorstarters en herintreders. (The fading line between work and pension)*, 2009, pp. 129.
77. Pearl A. Dykstra, *Ageing, intergenerational solidarity and age-specific vulnerabilities*, 2008, pp. 167.
76. Tineke Fokkema, Susan ter Bekke en Pearl A. Dykstra, *Solidarity between parents and their adult children in Europe*, 2008. pp. 125.
75. Harry van Dalen en Kène Henkens, *Weg uit Nederland: emigratie aan het begin van de 21e eeuw, (Leaving the Netherlands: Emigration at the start of the 21st century)*, 2008, pp. 134.

74. Harry van Dalen, Kène Henkens en Joop Schippers, *Oudere werknemers door de lens van de werkgever, (Older employees through the eyes of the employer),* 2007, pp. 122. € 11,50.

A NIDI report (1-74) can be ordered by remitting the amount due, plus postage and administrative costs (€ 5,00), to bank account number 45.83.68.687 (ABN-AMRO, The Hague) in the name of NIDI-KNAW, The Hague, mentioning the relevant report number with reference to the SWIFT-code: ABNANL2A and the IBAN-code: NL56ABNA0458368687. The address of the ABN-AMRO is P.O. BOX 90, 1000 AB in Amsterdam. If you wish to order more than one report, please telephone us (+31-70-3565200) as the editions are limited.
Report 75 et cetera can be ordered at Amsterdam University Press, Herengracht 221, 1016 BG Amsterdam, www.aup.nl

(Subject to changes)

For Product Safety Concerns and Information please contact our EU
representative GPSR@taylorandfrancis.com
Taylor & Francis Verlag GmbH, Kaufingerstraße 24, 80331 München, Germany

www.ingramcontent.com/pod-product-compliance
Lightning Source LLC
Chambersburg PA
CBHW050532270326
41926CB00015B/3186